CENTER AGAINST RAPE AND DOMESTIC VIOLENCE

24-hour Crisis and Support Line:
541-754-0110
800-927-0197

Advocacy Center:
2208 SW Third Street
Corvallis, Oregon
541-738-8319

Administrative Office:
4786 SW Philomath Boulevard
Corvallis, Oregon
541-758-0219

Mailing Address:
PO Box 914
Corvallis, Oregon 97339

Web Site:
www.cardv.org

CARDV provides services to survivors of domestic and sexual violence and their supporters regardless of race, gender identity, sexual orientation, ability, religion, class, ethnicity, age, or immigration status.

All services are free and confidential.

The Center Against Rape and Domestic Violence

A Local History of a National Movement

Mary Zelinka

MOTHER BADGER PRESS

Design by Meadowlark Publishing Services.

Unless otherwise noted, all illustrations are from the CARDV archives.

Published by Mother Badger Press
PO Box 3047
Albany, OR 97321
motherbadgerpress@gmail.com

Manufactured in the United States of America.
ISBN 978-0-9975405-0-5
Published 2016

To the bold and insistent women
who had the audacity to demand a better world.
And to all those who carry on what they started.

Never doubt that a small group of thoughtful,
committed citizens can change the world;
indeed, it's the only thing that ever has.
Margaret Mead

The violets in the mountains have broken the rocks.
Tennessee Williams

Contents

Part One: The Beginning. 1

June 1981 3

A Daunting Task 7

The Auspicious Beginning 21

From Radical Upstart to Community Leader. 37

Part Two: Operations. .53

Programs and Services .55

Funding. 81

Fundraising 91

Community Education .99

Facilities 105

Community Partnerships and Coalitions 111

Community Awareness. 121

Legislation 133

Part Three: The Future 145

Towards That Glorious Day 147

Photos. 163

Appendices. 197

    Power and Control Wheel 199

    Wheel of Equality 201

    The Center Against Rape and Domestic Violence
    Mission Statement and Principles of Unity 203

    Executive Directors 207

    Awards and Honors. 209

    CARDV Board of Directors. 213

Acknowledgments 223

Resources. 225

About the Author 233

Part One
The Beginning

June 1981

A t least twenty-five of us crowded into the Rape Crisis Center's office that sweltering summer evening. In spite of the importance of the task ahead of us, there was a lot of laughter, a combination of nervousness and excitement.

Two small rooms at the top of the stairs at 216 SW Madison Avenue in downtown Corvallis comprised the Rape Crisis Center. One room was crammed with desks, file cabinets and bookcases overflowing with books and binders. Stacks of paper covered every surface. Donated chairs arranged in a circle filled the second room which we used as a meeting space—metal folding chairs, swiveling desk chairs, and one shabby overstuffed chair hunched in the corner. A blackboard set on an easel leaned against one of the walls.

Posters, announcements, and cartoons papered the dingy walls. One I remember clearly: a little girl with long braids down her back holding a briefcase stands in front of a reception desk. The receptionist is speaking into a phone. She has a smirk on her face. "Sir, the 'girl' you requested from the agency is here." Years would pass before women would be routinely referred to as anything other than "girl" or "honey" or "sweetie" or "beautiful" or "darling."

We came together that night to name our new agency. The merger between the Rape Crisis Center and the Linn-Benton Association for the Prevention of Domestic Violence would be official the next month.

Everyone squeezed into the meeting room. There was probably air conditioning, but I remember it as being hot and foggy with smoke; just about everybody smoked back then. We perched on chairs, sat on the floor, leaned against the walls and the open doorways. Barb Sussex, director of the Rape Crisis Center, and Deb Ross, director of the Linn-Benton Association, stood in the corner with the blackboard, each with chalk in her hand.

With the exception of Barb and Deb and one half-time advocate, we were all volunteers. The majority of us were survivors—and some of us not very long away from abusive relationships or sexual assaults. By CARDV's current standards, many of us shouldn't have been doing direct service yet; we were still too close to our own crises. But if not us, then who?

Prior to our involvement with the Rape Crisis Center and the Association, most of us had no experience in making decisions, even in our personal lives. We had never held a position of authority, and we had not witnessed many women who had. Barb and Deb came the closest—being directors of two small, soon to be one, private non-profits. But outside our little group, their influence was dubious.

Neither agency had any clout in the community and the annual salary to be split between them after the merger, $13,494, wasn't even respectable.

Egged on by one another's passion, determination, and sometimes pure rage, we had disregarded our lack of experience and flung ourselves into formulating bylaws for our new agency, writing training materials and grants, and holding leadership positions at the Rape Crisis Center and the Linn-Benton Association. Now we were just months away from opening a shelter for survivors of domestic violence. Few of us had even heard of a domestic violence shelter until we joined this grassroots movement—the first in the country having opened just seven years before. Our shelter would be among the first of its kind in Oregon.

Our new agency's name would be chosen that night by consensus, the way we made all our decisions in those days, each woman having equal say.

We wanted a name that reflected what we stood for. One that a survivor would immediately recognize. Back then, the words "rape" and "domestic violence" were brash and shocking. Newspapers still reported rapes as "assaults" and domestic violence incidents were usually described as "lovers' quarrels."

We all agreed. Saying the words "rape" or "sexual assault" and "domestic violence" out loud takes the secrecy out of those issues. Euphemisms imply to survivors that they should be ashamed about what happened to them. If we don't say the words, how can a survivor? Being blunt and upfront forces the community to acknowledge what survivors have to live with every day.

Someone must have taken notes from that meeting. Years later I discovered a tattered file in a box marked "old shelter documents" in the CARDV administrative office's attic. Inside was a sheet of faded pink paper with a list of possible agency names. One name had a big star beside it: "The Center Against Rape and Domestic Violence."

The name was bold, revolutionary. A political statement.

If we hadn't already known it, by the end of that meeting we had no doubt—our work was changing the world. And changing each of us right along with it.

A Daunting Task

Violence against women was largely hidden until the 1970s. Domestic violence, sexual assault, incest, stalking, sexual harassment, being prostituted and used in pornography were for the most part all unspoken female experiences. If a woman did find the courage to speak up, most likely the legal and social response was that she herself was to blame. There were no rape crisis lines, no domestic violence shelters, no support groups.

The movement to end violence against women was a result of the second-wave feminist movement, grown out of the peace and civil rights movements of the 1960s. The women working for peace and civil rights realized that they were trying to obtain rights for others that they themselves did not have. Most women working for social change were cooking, typing, running errands, and performing other tasks their male co-workers assigned to them.

Though the Virginia Slims cigarette ads assured women

that "You've come a long way, baby," there was little proof of that actually being true. In the 1970s a woman was earning less than 59 cents to the dollar a man earned, and it was hard, if not impossible, for her to get credit in her own name. Depending upon what state she lived in, she wouldn't be able to sit on a jury until 1973. Job discrimination on the basis of gender was legal. When a woman interviewed for a job, she was typically given a typing test, and most often she was expected to quit working as soon as she got married. In the rare case that a woman became an executive, she was called a "lady boss."

Women grew up knowing their career options were limited—the primers they learned to read in as children had told them so. In the 1970s Margaret Lumpkin, professor at Oregon State University and one of the founders of Corvallis Women Against Rape, together with Gwyneth Britton, did extensive research in race and gender career stereotyping in children's public school primers. Their groundbreaking work discovered there were over 400 career opportunities mentioned for men and only five for women: mother, teacher, nurse, princess, and witch.

Most people believed that women were unable to cooperate with one another—that they would wind up competing with each other for a man's attention. The woman who didn't want to be a mother was labeled unnatural. If a man was violent toward a woman, she was either masochistic or had provoked him. If she was raped, she asked for it.

Women's dissatisfaction in the peace and civil rights movements led to consciousness-raising groups, which began springing up all over the country. These meetings typically involved going around the room and giving each woman the opportunity to speak about an issue in her own life. Sometimes topics were chosen: husbands or boyfriends, children, financial dependence, work. For the first time women began talking about the truth of their lives.

Before the 1970s, sexual matters hadn't been talked about openly and these social prohibitions on forthright language helped keep violence issues hidden. But the 1960s fostered conversations about sexual satisfaction, birth control and abortion, and in this new openness women began speaking about sexual and domestic violence.

And speak they did. The overwhelming theme of those consciousness-raising groups was one of violence: rape, battery, incest, stalking, sexual harassment, prostitution and pornography. The women talked about the violence they had experienced themselves, or had witnessed their mothers going through, or the events in their sisters' or friends' lives. And the more they talked, the angrier they became.

It was out of these consciousness-raising groups that the National Organization for Women (NOW) and the Women's Liberation Movement, as well as the Anti-Violence Movement, originated. The anti-violence movement and the feminist movement were linked both philosophically and politically. The feminist movement gave power and numbers and strength to the anti-violence movement and the anti-violence movement gave the feminist movement a sense of urgency.

It didn't matter how much money women made or whether they were called girls if they could be systematically battered and raped. What women realized in those consciousness-raising groups was that domestic violence and sexual assault wasn't an individual's problem, it was deeply rooted in our culture. One gender had power over another gender. And just as an abuser uses power and control over his victim, so domestic violence, sexual assault, stalking, prostitution, pornography and sexual harassment, or the threat of those things, control women. As Susan Brownmiller, author of *Against Our Will: Men, Women, and Rape,* would later say, "Rape is ... a conscious process of intimidation that keeps all women in a state of fear."

The power structures had to be changed or violence against women would never stop.

Not surprisingly, the backlash against feminism started at the same time as the second-wave feminist movement did. Vehement diatribes and ridicule were aimed against the women involved—all designed to discredit the movement and to discourage other women from joining. When Phyllis Schlafly, attorney and outspoken opponent of feminism said, "Women's liberation is a total assault on the role of the American woman as a wife and mother and on the family as the basic unit of society," most people agreed with her.

The Equal Rights Amendment became the focal point of the attack against the fledgling women's movement. The text of the proposed amendment is stated in full as follows:

Section 1. Equality of rights under the law shall not be denied or abridged by the United States or by any State on account of sex.

Section 2. The Congress shall have the power to enforce, by appropriate legislation, the provisions of this article.

Section 3. This amendment shall take effect two years after the date of ratification.

In 1972 both houses of Congress passed the amendment, but even with the deadline of 1979 extended four years to 1982, it was not ratified by the required number of states. The opposition's fear tactics had been successful: women would be drafted for combat service; women's privileges and protections would be taken away; the government would mandate all men's and women's restrooms to become unisex.

Pat Robertson would go a step further by declaring in a 1992 fundraising letter opposing a state equal-rights amendment in Iowa, "The feminist agenda is not about equal rights for women. It is about a socialist, anti-family political movement that encourages women to leave their husbands, kill their children, practice witchcraft, destroy capitalism and become lesbians."

Women's rights have never been freely given. The Suffragists had endured similar hostile reactions.

Just as the second-wave feminist movement grew out of the peace and civil rights movements, the female abolitionists of the nineteenth century had gone on to organize the Suffrage Movement. This first wave of feminism began in 1848 during the first women's rights convention in Seneca

Falls, NY. It would take seventy-two years for women to gain the right to vote in 1920.

Political cartoons of the time depicted the suffragists as ugly, old and unmarried women out to devalue men. Angry newspaper editorials declared that women's enfranchisement would create a role reversal and that men would have the same expectations of child rearing and homemaking placed upon them as women did. Suffragists were beaten; declared insane and committed to insane asylums on their husbands' authority; jailed; and force-fed. Women died trying to obtain the right to vote.

The suffrage movement came to a head on November 15, 1917, the "Night of Terror." Thirty-three demonstrators picketing Woodrow Wilson's White House with signs asking for the vote were jailed. Prison guards, with the warden's blessing, beat, kicked, and choked the women. Some were tortured. Two weeks later, a court-ordered hearing exposed the beaten women to the world and they were released.

The suffragists continued to picket the White House. When they were arrested, others came to take their place. It would take three more years to win the vote.

With more and more women joining or starting their own consciousness-raising groups in the 1970s, the accounts of violence multiplied. And with each report, the women's anger intensified. They decided to fight back. And they did by igniting a grassroots movement that created crisis lines and shelters for raped and battered women.

Rape hotlines started with women's home phone

numbers, with the first official rape crisis hotline beginning operation in St. Paul, Minnesota in 1972. Those early rape crisis centers were commonly acknowledged as being anti-establishment. This is hardly surprising since the "establishment" hadn't done anything to support rape survivors. Police officers routinely accused survivors of provoking their attack, and hospitals had no protocols in place for treating them. Rape crisis centers were at odds with most mainstream organizations.

In 1973 the Rape Relief Hotline (now Portland Women's Crisis Line) and Mid-Valley Women's Crisis Service (now Center for Hope and Safety in Salem) opened Oregon's first hotlines.

Shelters for women fleeing violence had long existed, but they were accessible only if the woman in need knew who to approach. This in itself could place her in danger. Well into the mid-twentieth century, husbands could have their wives committed to insane asylums based on little more authority than their own word. Until the early twentieth century, if women divorced, they lost all rights to their children. Divorce was granted only under limited circumstances, such as "extreme cruelty" until the 1970s.

Susan B. Anthony, among many other suffragists and abolitionists, sheltered women in her home during the mid-1800's and participated in helping women flee violent marriages through a network of homes operating similarly to how the Underground Railroad helped slaves escape.

The first domestic violence shelters were in family or friends' houses, or in the living rooms of women that the survivor had just met. Some shelters evolved seemingly all on their own, as in the many cases where a newly single mom would put an ad in the paper for a roommate and

find that the women responding were fleeing violent relationships. Soon the single mom would be housing a dozen
or more women.

Early shelters advocated for an egalitarian communal
structure—women helping women. Erin Pizzey, author of
the 1974 groundbreaking book *Scream Quietly or the Neigh-
bors Will Hear*, opened the first battered women's shelter
in England in 1971. Begun as a daytime women's center,
within a year thirty-four women and children were living
in the house. The women themselves were answering the
hotline and providing support for one another.

The first official battered women's shelter opened in the
United States in St. Paul, Minnesota in 1974. Bradley-Angle
House in Portland would follow just two years later in 1976
as the first domestic violence shelter in Oregon and on the
West Coast.

From the very beginning, it was understood that the
shelters needed to blend into neighborhoods and be
secreted from batterers and the public. Additionally, they
should be run by women for women, and as collectively as
possible.

Critics blamed feminism for the violence against women.
They pointed out that roles between men and women
were not so easily defined as they had been in the past:
women were working outside the home and demanding
equal rights. While women have always been blamed for
having been sexually assaulted, now feminism was being
blamed right along with them for encouraging women
to wear what they were comfortable wearing and going

where they wanted to go. A 1968 Harris poll found that 20 percent approved of slapping one's spouse on "appropriate occasions."

Violence against women has been with us through the ages. What the feminist movement did was challenge the belief systems that had condoned that violence.

Throughout much of recorded history, women and children were considered property of their husbands or fathers. The word "family" comes from the Latin word "familia," meaning servant, slave, possession. When a woman married, ownership transferred to the husband. The father or husband had absolute control.

In Biblical times if a man raped a virgin and it was within the walls of the city, the elders reasoned that if she had screamed, someone would have rescued her, therefore both the virgin and the rapist shared the same fate—death by stoning. If the rape took place outside the city, her screams might not have been heard. So the rapist was ordered to pay the girl's father fifty silver shekels in compensation for what would have been her bride price, and the pair was commanded to wed.

The early settlers in North America adopted the English Common Law, "Rule of Thumb," which permitted wife-beating for "correctional purposes" as long as the "rod was not thicker than his thumb or longer than his forearm."

In 1874, The Supreme Court of North Carolina held "the husband has no right to chastise his wife under any circumstances," but "if no permanent injury has been inflicted … it is better to … leave the parties to forget and forgive."

Women who fought back were vilified, as in the case of Charity Lamb, who struck her husband in the skull with an axe. In 1854 she became the first woman to be convicted of murder in Oregon Territory. In spite of two of her children testifying that their father had kicked and beaten their mother with his fists, struck her with a hammer, and threatened her with guns, she was found guilty of second-degree murder. Newspapers of the day declared her a "monster" and "inhuman." Sentenced to the all-male prison in Portland, she was later transferred to Hawthorne's Insane Asylum where she died in 1879.

Feminists began publishing articles and books about violence against women in the 1970s, fueling the anti-violence movement.

Ms. Magazine published their inaugural issue in July 1972. The first magazine of its kind, mainstream media ridiculed the effort and gave it six months before it folded. Critics pointed out that women wanted to read about fashion, makeup and hair styling, and improving their relationships — not politics. *Ms.* would be the first national magazine to discuss domestic violence when it published a revolutionary cover story in 1976. The 1977 *Ms.* cover story, "Sexual Harassment on the Job and How to Stop It," preceded the Supreme Court's 1986 decision that sexual harassment creates a hostile work environment, thereby violating the law. *Ms.* reported on the prevalence of sexual assault against college women in 1985 and commissioned a national study of date rape.

Susan Brownmiller's *Against Our Will: Men, Women and Rape,* published in 1975, and Del Martin's 1976 *Battered Wives* were the go-to books in the anti-violence movement.

Besides providing an historical context for violence against women, the books were major sources of information. Both Brownmiller and Martin were clear—rape and battery would continue as long as gender inequality existed.

Aegis Magazine on Ending Violence Against Women, from Feminist Alliance Against Rape, provided grassroots domestic and sexual violence agencies with invaluable practical information and resources.

Andrea Dworkin, anti-pornography activist, published *Woman Hating* in 1974 and *Pornography: Men Possessing Women* in 1981, amongst many other publications. Until her death in 2005, Dworkin would write, speak, and seek to pass legislation against pornography which she maintained was directly linked to rape and the subjugation of women.

In 1979 Lenore Walker published *The Battered Woman.* The "cycle of violence" she used to describe a batterer's violent behavior was initially widely acclaimed and used extensively by domestic violence advocates. Years later, after advocates gained more experience, the model's inaccuracies surfaced and was finally discontinued. Walker's cycle provided that invaluable starting point for future research to build upon.

Sex Crimes, published in 1993 by Alice Vachss, former Chief of the Special Victims Bureau in the Queens District Attorney's Office in New York City, exposed a legal system weighted against rape survivors. Vachss charged that police officers, prosecutors, and judges all too often gave the rapist a break, therefore acting as "rape collaborators."

~

The battered women's movement was a tough setting to work in—many believed it to be the most difficult of all the feminist causes. The burnout rate was significant. The work was not simply about creating and providing services for survivors, that in itself a monumental task. It was also about changing the attitudes that had fostered the violence in the first place.

Rapists and batterers had to be held accountable; laws needed to be changed; law enforcement and district attorneys had to be better informed; hospitals needed procedures in place to serve rape survivors; schools and communities required education. Eons of gender conditioning had to be overcome—for both women and men.

Language had to be addressed. Too many words that included both women and men referenced only men, such as mankind, manmade, manpower, forefathers. Women needed to be included in job titles—mailman, policeman, fireman, handyman—prefacing the position with a "lady" or "girl" wasn't good enough. Violent metaphors in our everyday language were so prevalent few people even noticed them: "Getting away with murder," "killing time," "when push comes to shove," "killing them with kindness," "screaming bloody murder."

Thinly veiled hostile humor about women needed to be confronted—dumb blonde and mother-in-law jokes; stories and puns about rape and battery; sexist skits. Women's portrayal in movies, television, and popular music reinforced negative stereotypes of women and romanticized women being prostituted. Advertising depicted women as being either nurturing mother figures or sex objects wanting to be dominated by men.

For anyone working in the movement, there was no question—violence against women was directly related to how the culture viewed women. And changing those deeply rooted cultural norms was fundamental in ending that violence. It was a daunting task.

The Auspicious Beginning

CWAR AND THE RAPE CRISIS CENTER

In 1975, the Sunflower House (Community Outreach, Inc.) operated its mostly volunteer-run general hotline out of a room no bigger than a closet on the Oregon State University campus. Margaret Lumpkin, Oregon State University professor and one of the founders of Sunflower House, noticed that the majority of calls coming in were from women and were about rape. She also observed that the survivors didn't want to talk to the male volunteers — they wanted to talk to another woman.

Lumpkin talked to some of her friends and a few months later, on March 19, 1976, Corvallis Women Against Rape (CWAR), run entirely by volunteers, was incorporated.

CWAR's hotline opened without any fanfare on Friday, January 14, 1977, a week before Jimmy Carter would be sworn in as President of the United States. The *Corvallis*

Gazette-Times ran an article announcing the hotline, but it's doubtful that very many people gave it much thought. That Friday night Linn and Benton county residents were unwinding after a long week and planning their weekends. Many were probably watching *Charlie's Angels* on television or reading Alex Haley's *Roots*.

No one, not even the volunteers at CWAR, suspected that a force had just been set in motion that would ultimately change how law enforcement, courts, local government, medical professionals, social service agencies, schools, newspapers, businesses, and community members would respond to sexual assault survivors.

The concept of sexual assault services was new to CWAR volunteers as well. There were no established trainings to attend, no professional conferences. CWAR volunteers created services as they went along. They listened to the callers and asked what they could do to help. Most of the volunteers were survivors themselves and tried to give the same kind of support they wished they had gotten.

Without realizing it, CWAR had stumbled onto the foundation of advocacy: It is only the present circumstances that separate us. They listened carefully to the survivor's needs and made no judgments about her. What had happened to the caller, or the survivor they were meeting at the hospital, could just as easily have happened to them. As often it had. A mantra in the movement became "always believe the survivor." This, the volunteers did instinctively.

Initially the hotline was operational from 7:00 p.m. Friday evenings until 7:00 a.m. Sunday mornings. The phone number, 754-0110, is the same crisis line number CARDV continues to answer today.

CWAR's immediate goals were to increase coverage to twenty-four hours, seven days a week, and to guarantee that a woman would always answer the telephone. In 1978 CWAR answered 349 calls and performed thirty-three speaking engagements with over 1,000 people in attendance.

Volunteers put CWAR posters up throughout Linn and Benton counties to advertise the hotline, and did radio interviews. They designed trainings and presented them to law enforcement and the hospitals, went to NOW (National Organization for Women) meetings, wrote to Congress, and attended grant writing workshops. They met with the district attorneys to find out why rape charges were routinely plea bargained down. They talked to judges. And they cheered when, in 1978, Oregon became the first state to pass legislation making marital rape a crime.

By January 1979 CWAR was looking to hire someone to write grants, schedule volunteers, plan for volunteer trainings, and respond to speaking requests, as well as oversee all administrative tasks and cover the hotline when volunteers weren't available. Hotline hours steadily increased until, by 1980, it was finally available twenty-four hours a day, seven days a week.

In May of 1979, CWAR officially changed their name to the Rape Crisis Center. There is no record of why. A common name of the early rape crisis centers around the country at that time was the hotline's location followed by "Women Against Rape." By the late 1970s many groups began changing their names. It's possible that CWAR adopted "Rape Crisis Center" to acknowledge that their service area was larger than just Corvallis.

Barb Sussex, the Rape Crisis Center's first director and

first paid staff, was essential to the grassroots organization, but far more was needed than just one person could keep up with. Volunteers were crucial—all hotline and in-person response shifts were covered by volunteers from 5:00 p.m. to 8:00 a.m. weekdays and weekends from 5:00 p.m. Fridays to 8:00 a.m. Mondays. Volunteers facilitated support groups; spoke to schools or community groups when Sussex was unavailable; assisted with grant writing; wrote letters to the editors of local newspapers; staffed booths at fairs; handed out leaflets on street corners. They attended a volunteer meeting every week to review hotline and hospital calls, and to sign up for shifts for the coming week. And they filled the two slots on the Board of Directors reserved for volunteers actively doing direct services. As one volunteer put it, "You don't just volunteer at the Rape Crisis Center, you adopt a way of life."

Volunteers also helped Sussex with the never-ending office work. Letters, grants, brochures, and newsletters had to be typed either on the Rape Crisis Center's manual typewriter, or taken home and typed on the volunteers'. Support group flyers were hand-drawn and copied.

Sections of the volunteer manual were divided up among volunteers to be typed on stencils and run off on a mimeograph machine. The week before a training began, volunteers gathered after work to collate the new manuals. Piles of the purple-inked pages were stacked on the floor along the walls in the dimly lit corridor outside the Rape Crisis Center's tiny offices, the air thick with the heady smell of mimeograph ink. Laughing and talking non-stop, volunteers walked up and down the hall, taking a page from each pile until the manuals were assembled.

After meetings, the volunteers who didn't have to rush

home to cover a hotline shift gathered at Squirrels Tavern to swap stories from their own lives. The confidence they were gaining through their work at the Rape Crisis Center gave them a different sense of who they were and how they expected to be treated in the world. They carried this new self-assurance into their jobs and personal lives. When they told a hotline caller "you don't deserve to be treated like that," some of them realized they should be telling themselves the exact same thing about their own relationships. The volunteers were changing and growing right along with the grassroots movement they were immersed in. Many became life-long friends.

LINN-BENTON ASSOCIATION FOR THE PREVENTION OF DOMESTIC VIOLENCE

After a discussion of child abuse and domestic violence at the Council of Social Agencies meeting in October 1978, a suggestion was made that someone should explore the feasibility of a shelter for battered women. Several people met the next month to continue this conversation. They designed a form to collect statistics and invited Bradley-Angle House in Portland, the first domestic violence shelter in Oregon and on the West Coast, to a meeting in December.

Statistics obtained through area law enforcement and local social services agencies, including CWAR, Sunflower House, FISH, Linn County Children's Services, and Legal Aid, convinced the group to continue. The 1978 domestic violence responses in Benton County totaled 297 and in Linn County 610.

The grassroots group incorporated as the Linn-Benton Association for the Prevention of Domestic Violence on May 18, 1979. Benton County provided the Association 100 square feet of office space at no charge in the Corvallis Human Resources Center at 850 SW 35th Street. The phone number, 758-0219, is still the general office number to CARDV's administrative office today.

The Association took stock of what services were available in Linn and Benton counties for women escaping violence in their home. The list was pretty short. A couple of private homes were available as temporary safe houses through a religious service provider, FISH Guest House, but stays were limited to one or two nights and there was no link with other services.

The Sunflower House had a system in place. Their 1979 report to the Association states, "If a woman wants to get out of the home immediately, the Mobile Crisis Intervention Team, consisting of a male and a female, will go to the residence or designated meeting place and assist the victim in getting out. If the potential for danger from weapons is thought to be high then we may elect to call in the police. They will talk to both people involved and remove the woman if necessary. It might be that the couple does not want to separate but needs some counseling to help work out their problems. We will do some immediate problem solving and then refer them to an appropriate counselor for ongoing help. If the woman does wish to be removed we will bring her back to Sunflower House and help her deal with her emotional concerns. We will also locate a temporary place to stay ..."

The temporary places to stay were the safe houses, consisting of a small network of community members' homes. And they were lifesaving. But the stays were just for one to three days, not nearly long enough for a survivor to make important life decisions, secure financial assistance, take care of her children's needs, and find a place to live.

There was no training available for the hosts of the safe houses. Their names and phone numbers were placed on a list and they were called, usually at night, before a survivor and her children were brought. When they were dropped off, the survivor was told that the location had to be kept confidential. Sometimes the survivor stayed up through the night talking with the host, sometimes she just wanted to go to her room and sleep.

Services for battered women were a new concept, the terms "battered woman" and "domestic violence" were not even part of the public's vocabulary yet. The National Office of Violence Against Women, which provides technical assistance and training to domestic violence programs throughout the country, wouldn't exist for another sixteen years; "best practices" and "trauma-informed services," common terms today, were twenty years away.

Like all of the early programs around the country, the Association and the Rape Crisis Center saw a need, didn't know how to fill that need, and then filled it anyway. Future "best practices" would have their origins in those early grassroots efforts.

Bradley-Angle House's domestic violence training for the Association in 1979 would teach them that some of the services currently being provided in the community might be detrimental to the safety of the survivors. Couples counseling, for instance, thought by many at the time to be a logical step in resolving difficulties, could place the survivor in greater danger. In domestic violence, characterized by power and control by the abuser, anything the survivor said in counseling could, and probably would, be used against her.

From the Association's very first meeting their primary mission was to purchase a safe house for battered women. With $377.97 in the bank they began looking for suitable houses.

Until a shelter became available, the Association worked on designing services. Support groups were offered in Albany and Sweet Home for "battered women and threatened women." With a donation from a local women's service club, they developed a card for law enforcement to carry describing a woman's legal rights. The Association's name was next to the Sheriff Office's name and phone number. Monthly newsletters—a five- to six-page single-spaced missive typed on a stencil, run off on a mimeograph machine and assembled by hand—kept subscribers updated on the Association's progress. Subscriptions were available to the public for the price of the yearly dues for membership in the Association: $3.00 for individuals, $5.00 for organizations and families.

The Association had plenty of people interested in attending the planning meetings, but they were desperate for volunteers to work with survivors and provide safe houses. In spite of their advertising efforts only one safe house was available in Linn County and just a few in Benton. Volunteers were just as scarce, despite the trainings offered by the Association at Linn-Benton Community College.

The Association didn't hire an employee, Deb Ross

who was initially part-time, until January 1980. From 8:00 to 5:00 Monday through Friday, survivors could call either the Association office or Adult and Family Services (now Department of Human Services) Volunteer Services and speak to an advocate. After hours, the Sunflower House general hotline was available.

By February 1980, the Association had five active volunteers. Advocates discussed options with women: "separation injunction, divorce, public benefits, food, education, and housing information." They provided transportation to doctors' offices and lawyers, or met the women at their appointments. Every month there were more clients—six, then seven, ten, sixteen.

Ross met with newspapers again and again until they published articles about the organization and the issue of domestic violence. She spoke on local radio stations to inform the public about the services available for battered women and the services needed. And the services needed far outweighed the services available. Besides the lack of a confidential shelter, safe houses and advocates, Oregon Legal Services was forced to cut back on the number of domestic violence related cases they were taking. They simply did not have the necessary resources.

Lack of services, volunteers, safe houses, and finances didn't dampen the Association's determination to acquire a confidential shelter. With a budget for fiscal year 1979–1980 of $1,150, which included proceeds from a garage sale and a Benton County Fair joint BINGO fundraiser with Sunflower House, they continued looking for houses.

In July of 1980, the Association submitted a Community Development Block Grant proposal to the City of Corvallis for a confidential shelter. Their eloquent grant request

provided the City with what was probably their first education about domestic violence: "Many victims will stay in
violent situations because they have no other place to go.
In response to this, Sunflower House developed a small
private home network to house victims. The usual period
of time clients can stay in these safe homes is one to three
days. This network helps meet some very immediate housing needs of domestic violence victims, but falls short when
considering the client's other crucial needs. First, a few
days is not enough time to make important life decisions,
secure financial assistance, take care of their children's concern and confusion, and find an apartment. Secondly, it is
very difficult for advocates to work with clients when they
do not have a secure place to meet. Advocate/client contact
is very important in the first days of this transitional time.
Without this needed support, many women go back to the
violent situation because the changes required to live a life
without violence seem too overwhelming."

While the Association waited to hear from the City
about the CDBG grant, they applied to a savings and loan
bank for a loan to purchase a home downtown. Their
request was declined.

In December 1980, the Association and the Rape Crisis
Center began discussions about the possibility of a combined crisis line, joint training and a shared office. There
was a lot of overlap of services since the majority of sexual
assaults are committed by someone the victim either knows
or is in relationship with. And sexual assault is a common
tactic abusers use to control their victims.

The City of Corvallis approved the Community Development Block Grant application in February 1981. A grant
of $70,000 to $100,000 was allocated, to be made available

in October. Though the decision was unanimous, the City expressed concerns that the Association didn't have the funding to staff and operate the shelter. They had good reason to be concerned—the Association had a bank balance of $129.65 at the time, one staff person, and only five direct service volunteers.

Merging the Association and the Rape Crisis Center plans moved forward while the two agencies searched for suitable houses and discussed shelter services.

There was no question in either the Association or the Rape Crisis Center's minds that the shelter's location should be kept confidential. The Benton County Sheriff's Office agreed, citing national statistics that 40 percent of police calls were related to domestic violence and 20 percent of police deaths were a result of responding to those calls.

The Association/Rape Crisis Center mailed sixty-eight surveys to domestic violence shelters around the country soliciting input on shelter policies. Of particular interest concerned older boy children. Most shelters, they found, had strict age limits on boys admitted. After much discussion, everyone agreed: the older boys got, the more likely they were to use violence themselves; and it might be upsetting to the other women to have an older boy in the close communal living quarters. It was decided to set the limit at age twelve, but "take each case individually," a decision that CARDV would be challenged by until the year 2000 when policies were changed to accept male survivors of any age.

Two possible houses were identified and a special meeting was held on July 8, 1981 with the directors and boards of the Association and the Rape Crisis Center to choose between them. All were in favor of the red brick "highway" house except for one who voted for the "downtown" house and one who abstained.

THE CENTER AGAINST RAPE AND DOMESTIC VIOLENCE

The Association moved their office to the Rape Crisis Center's site at 216 SW Madison Avenue in Corvallis as the two agencies began the merger process.

A small committee consisting of the directors of the Rape Crisis Center and the Association, a board member who served on the boards for both agencies, and five Rape Crisis volunteers established key recommendations for board and volunteer approval. Central issues discussed were: the importance of maintaining a feminist philosophy; belief that the new agency should be run by women for women; callers should always reach a woman when calling the hotline; decisions should be made by consensus and by volunteers; and preserving the agencies' grassroots heritage.

Rape Crisis volunteers worried that sexual assault response would get downgraded or lost completely amidst the complexity of operating a domestic violence shelter. This would prove a legitimate concern, as years later, many dual programs providing both domestic violence and sexual assault services grappled with that very issue. CARDV made the commitment from the onset that all advocates would be as highly trained in responding to sexual assault as they were in domestic violence.

What would not become fully apparent until after the

merger was the fundamental dissimilarity of the two agencies. Like most of the early rape crisis centers, the Rape Crisis Center had operated outside of the mainstream and was frequently at odds with the system. Early members of the Association, on the other hand, came out of social service agencies and so from the beginning had experienced more acceptance within the community.

Another big difference was governance. The Rape Crisis Center's board of directors acted as an advisory board, with the volunteers setting policy. The Association's board made all major decisions and governed the director.

And perhaps most significant of all, the Rape Crisis Center was adamant that social change was imperative to ending violence against women. While many Association members agreed and even asserted at community speaking events, the closest they came as an agency to a public declaration was their statement, "domestic violence is still seldom viewed as a serious social problem."

Throughout the merger discussions, a great deal of energy was spent trying to create a structure that represented everyone—to maintain volunteer leadership and ensure that women who were impacted by violence had a voice. Ultimately, the merger was successful because however different the two agencies were, each absolutely believed that domestic and sexual violence was never the victim's fault. Rather, it was firmly entrenched in our culture which granted one gender power over another.

In July, a week after the new agency was named the Center Against Rape and Domestic Violence, the following

Mission Statement and Principles of Unity were adopted unanimously by volunteers, staff and board with the pronouncement: "This statement shall serve as the new Corporation's statement of philosophy and no policy shall violate these principles."

Mission:

The purpose of this corporation is to provide immediate assistance to victims of domestic and sexual violence and to change societal conditions that cause that violence to exist. To this end, the following principles have been adopted:

Principles of Unity:

Victimization of Women

We believe that violence against women is endemic in our society. By "violence against women" we refer to both specific and general abuse of women in this society. In addition to murder, rape, battering, sexual harassment, pornography and other forms of physical violence, it also includes attitudes and values that create and reproduce violence. We believe that the root causes of this violence stem from a belief in the supremacy of one sex over the other and are legitimated and reproduced by a complex series of institutional and social arrangements that define and treat women as subordinate.

Freedom from Violation

We believe that all women have the right to live a life free of violence or the threat of violence. They have the right to freedom from violations of their personal autonomy and physical integrity on the street, in the home and at the workplace. To insure this, women should not have to restrict their freedom of movement, their bodies or their activities in order to be safe.

Self-Determination

We believe that all women have the right to make their own decisions regarding sexual and reproductive matters, lifestyles, finances, education and employment.

Religious Freedom

Religious beliefs and practices are a matter of personal conscience and individual choice, and a member shall neither promote nor discourage a particular religious belief in the course of her/his work.

~

The Center Against Rape and Domestic Violence was officially incorporated on July 30, 1981.

Less than six months afterwards, on January 17, 1982, staff and volunteers hauled an impressive collection of mismatched donated furniture into the red brick "highway" house. And just days later survivors of domestic and sexual violence began finding refuge within the safety of its walls.

The red brick house would serve as a confidential shelter for over eighteen years. Nearly 5,000 women and children would be sheltered there by the time it was converted to CARDV's administrative offices in 2000.

From Radical Upstart
to Community Leader

F eminism was the ideal we clung to while we navigated those first confusing and uncertain years as we defined our new agency's culture and established ourselves in the community. At its most basic, feminism is about securing for women the same economic, political and social rights and protections that men enjoy. It is about expanding opportunities for women, not making choices for them. Which is the very essence of advocacy.

We were sensitive to power structures and imbalances — sexual and domestic violence were crimes of power and control. The "power over" structure that for the most part dominated society had left women and other marginal groups oppressed. We did everything we could to minimize the power imbalances between us and the survivors we worked with. And we wanted to do the same within our organization with one another.

We read *Values Clarification* (Simon, Howe and Kirschenbaum) and *No Bosses Here* (Brandon and McDonnell). We sat through hours-long meetings at night in the office or at one another's homes, appointing a facilitator to ensure that each person would be heard. We endured seemingly endless discussions: Should CARDV operate as a collective or a hierarchy; what role should men play in the agency; should differences in salary be based on skill or need?

In time we would come to understand that while those conversations rarely resolved anything, it was the act of having the discussions that was important. We were learning to say the things out loud that were significant to us. We were learning how to honor what others were saying, while at the same time disagreeing. We were learning how to trust each other and more importantly, ourselves.

There was no pattern for us to follow. We wanted to change how the world was working, but we didn't have an alternate model to change it to. What we wanted—a world where women were respected and not systematically sexually, physically, emotionally, or financially abused—was so drastically different from the world we inhabited that sometimes we didn't even know how to articulate it.

The work we were doing with survivors was extraordinarily hard. With no definitive organizational structure in place to keep us grounded, only the shining light of our Principles of Unity guided us. We were often unsure what, exactly, the role of CARDV was, or of our own roles as advocates. When issues arose in the agency that seemed insurmountable, we often reverted to the coping and problem-solving mechanisms we had been socialized with because that was what we knew best. At low points we took our frustrations out on each other. And when we did, we believed we had failed as advocates.

We would later learn that social change groups are hardest on themselves. No one expects a manufacturing plant or an insurance agency to be feminist-run, so when they behave in a less than stellar manner, no one believes they've failed their mission. The stakes are much higher for groups doing social change work. We held ourselves to an impossible standard.

Additionally, for the first year or two after the merger, volunteers grappled with the agency's new leadership structure. In the Rape Crisis Center, volunteers had been interchangeable with staff, but now, with the board setting policy and governing staff, volunteers assumed a lesser role. More paid staff were necessary when the shelter opened. Volunteers continued doing a large portion of the direct service—covering the hotline weekday evenings and overnights, as well as weekends. But as volunteer responsibilities dropped off, so did their involvement, and more and more of those overnight phone shifts had to be absorbed into staff duties.

Whatever form CARDV's growing pains took, our commitment to survivors never faltered.

We swapped shelter guidelines with the few other domestic violence shelters around the state and country, but basically we made up services as we went along, just as the other shelters were doing. If something worked, we kept doing it. If it didn't, we tried something else.

A live-in shelter advocate seemed like a good idea when the shelter first opened, but she only lasted a few months because she never got any time off. A rotation of overnight staff was put into place. Our policy regarding smoking developed after the night a shelter resident fell asleep with a lit cigarette. When the screeching smoke detector woke her and startled the whole house into action, the overnight volunteer stuffed the smoldering pillow into the kitchen sink and left the faucet drizzling over it through the night. Designated smoking areas were then assigned in shelter, and still later, moved outside.

We listened to shelter residents and tried to provide the services they needed, within the confines of a very limited budget. We vacillated between having strict boundaries with survivors and trying to do everything for them. We wanted to empower our clients to make decisions for themselves, but truthfully, most of us were still learning to do that ourselves. We had to be reminded more than once not to give out our personal phone numbers.

Sometimes in our zeal to right at least a few of the wrongs that had been done to our residents, we blatantly disregarded the policies CARDV had formulated for very good reasons, and risked our own safety. Stern lectures from Peter Sandrock, Benton County District Attorney at the time, reminded us that some situations were better left for law enforcement.

We accompanied shelter residents to medical appointments, restraining order hearings, and to the police station to file reports. We held sleeping children on our laps while they completed apartment applications. We laughed, raged, and grieved with them as we inserted pieces into the jigsaw puzzles they assembled on the shelter's dining room table. We sat with them on the shelter's back porch, talking and smoking and eating cookies late into the night. We bore witness to their fears and humiliations and pain.

~

In the 1980s the staff/volunteer phone lists and many of the board minutes recorded only first names. We were told not to use our last names because of "angry abusers who might want to get even."

There may have been another good reason for sticking to first names. In 2002 a *Portland Tribune* article reported that thirty-six boxes "stuffed with surveillance photographs, index cards, news clippings and intelligence reports collected between 1965 and the early 1980s were found in the garage of a retired Portland police officer." Bonnie Tinker, founder of the Rape Relief Hotline (now Portland Women's Crisis Line) and the Bradley-Angle House in Portland, was the subject of one of those files. The officer's 1979 report suggested Tinker planned to hide fugitives in the domestic violence shelter, and that the hotline was nothing more than an undercover message system.

The distrust of CARDV was palpable throughout much of the community—a fact that left at least one board member unperturbed. As she said, "We are working for social change. If we aren't making somebody mad at us, we're not doing our job." We were challenging the status quo and everything we did was suspect.

If we were strident and outraged in those days, it was because we didn't think others were paying attention or angry enough. While most agreed that it was absolutely disgraceful to rape or batter, few were willing to accept that the root cause of domestic and sexual violence was sexism. The majority of people believed it was a family problem and encouraged counseling for the offender. Far too many blamed the survivor for the violence.

We devoted much energy to educating law enforcement and the district attorneys. And we acquired some crucial supporters. In 1983 District Attorney Peter Sandrock copied CARDV on a memo he sent to all Benton County law enforcement agencies noting that the Oregon Supreme Court held that a peace officer is strictly liable for damages if he/she fails to make an arrest for a violation of a temporary restraining order issued under the Abuse Prevention Act. Sandrock added, "Please note that the duty to arrest for a TRO violation requires that you search out and arrest the suspect even if he is no longer at the scene of the domestic disturbance."

The Benton County Sheriff's Office called us to compare statistics. Deputy Stan Robson, later to become Benton County Sheriff, served on CARDV's Board of Directors just as he had for the Rape Crisis Center and the Linn-Benton Association for the Prevention of Domestic Violence. Deputy Robson saw CARDV as a key ally in his work with child sex abuse cases.

Linn County Sheriff's Deputy Art Martinak, later to become Sheriff, was active in the Linn-Benton Association for the Prevention of Domestic Violence from the beginning.

Faye Blake, from the City of Corvallis and one of CARDV's board members, reinforced our values: "… there is presently a lot of pressure from the community that CARDV mold itself to become like other local service organizations and … it is important for us not to yield to this pressure." Many agencies were providing invaluable services in the community, but none of them were doing anything about changing the societal conditions their clients had to live in. We wanted to put ourselves out of business.

CARDV kept repeating the hard facts of the dynamics of domestic and sexual violence wherever we spoke in the community. We did not soften our message or apologize for saying things that were uncomfortable for people to hear. We wrote letters to the editors of the newspapers in Linn and Benton counties and requested that the newspapers publish articles about the services we offered.

Over time, community members responded by going to CARDV's fund-raisers, bringing donations for the shelter, and writing us checks. People attended the trainings we presented at service organizations and invited us to speak at their own groups. Local musicians and businesses held benefits on our behalf. Seniors crocheted afghans for our shelter residents and children gave us toys and picture books they had outgrown.

The whole country was becoming more aware. Mainstream movies such as *The Burning Bed* (1984), *Extremities* (1986), and *The Accused* (1988) gave viewers a sense of the reality many survivors had experienced. Afternoon television talk show hosts like Oprah Winfrey discussed domestic violence, sexual assault, childhood sexual abuse, stalking, and sex trafficking. The silence surrounding violence against women had been shattered.

In 1991, Anita Hill's testimony before the Senate Judiciary Committee on Clarence Thomas's nomination to the Supreme Court, educated the entire nation about sexual harassment. Though Thomas was ultimately confirmed, the public debate the hearings generated forever changed how sexual harassment would be tolerated.

Then, beginning in 1994, the nation sat glued to their televisions for almost a full year watching the O. J. Simpson trial for the murders of his former wife, Nicole Brown Simpson, and her friend, Ronald Lyle Goldman.

During both Anita Hill's testimony and the Simpson trial, CARDV's hotline calls skyrocketed. Callers sought resources to help with the sexual harassment they were experiencing at work. Survivors reported their abusers were threatening to "O. J. them."

Backlash was inevitable.

Studies such as the Murray Straus and Richard Gelles research in the late 1980s claimed that domestic violence was gender-neutral. Their findings, based on a one-year time frame, likened a defensive slap by a woman to a man's punch that caused permanent injury. Though the Straus/Gelles research ignored the fact that domestic violence programs were quoting statistics from the FBI, the Department of Justice, the U.S. Surgeon General, the American Medical Association, and other organizations seldom credited for their feminist leanings, many believed the Straus/Gelles findings. To this day their research is still used to discredit survivors' experiences.

The backlash didn't stop with statistics. During the late 1990s, multiple lawsuits by accused perpetrators around the country charged psychiatrists and psychologists with propagating memories of childhood sexual abuse, incest and satanic ritual abuse in their patients — the "False Memory Syndrome." What was far more likely, of course, was that as an individual worked with a therapist through such issues as suicidal feelings, depression and eating disorders, memories of childhood sexual abuse surfaced.

The backlash had an enormous impact on survivors who were already blaming themselves for their abuse. CARDV overnight advocates could count on multiple hot-line calls each night from survivors questioning their own memories.

As technology evolved, so did CARDV. A brand new black IBM Selectric typewriter replaced the manual typewriter in the office in 1982, and in 1983 Hewett-Packard initiated CARDV into the computer age by donating an HP-87 computer with an ink jet printer. They even included a technician to train staff how to use it. By the early 2000's, CARDV was as dependent upon computers as any other organization.

In September 1994, US West began offering Caller ID in Linn and Benton counties. The new technology meant that survivors could no longer contact their abusers or their family and friends without revealing their whereabouts. We immediately blocked all CARDV's phone lines as well as our own, as sometimes we answered the hotline and called survivors from home. Attempts to block the lines of neighboring businesses, whose phones our shelter residents sometimes used, were unsuccessful.

Caller ID was just a forewarning of what was to come. The same technology designed to make communication more efficient also made stalking easier for abusers. Now they didn't have to leave their homes in order to stalk their victims. Hidden cameras, cell phone family locator services, GPS devices, even social media all rendered survivors more vulnerable.

The events of 9/11 impacted CARDV clients as well. Greyhound bus drivers began checking passengers' picture identification, making it harder for a survivor to leave town and start over again somewhere else. Though even in a new location anonymity doesn't last long. As soon as she accesses services and her personal information goes into the system, she becomes susceptible to tracking.

Safety planning with survivors today is far more complex than it was in the early days; now the whereabouts of the abuser is just the starting point.

As more sexual and domestic violence agencies developed around the state and country, advocates shared knowledge with one another, at first informally, and then through local and statewide trainings. CARDV advocates attended those first Oregon Coalition Against Sexual and Domestic Violence conferences in the 1980s hoping to hear from the experts. They were surprised to discover that they already knew as much as the experts did.

Based on our growing knowledge from working with survivors, CARDV advocates held trainings for judges and attorneys, law enforcement, medical personnel and nursing students, dentists and dental assistants, hair dressers, teachers, drug and alcohol counselors, and social workers. Students from Oregon State University's counseling and public health programs did internships at CARDV to learn about the impact of sexual and domestic violence on survivors.

Over time, state-wide trainings for advocates grew from three-day campouts at Girl Scout camps to professional conferences at convention centers featuring national speakers. National research better informed CARDV and other agencies around the country, and "best practices" became standards we aspired to in our service delivery. Webinars (seminars offered over the internet) now make it possible for advocates to attend national trainings at no cost.

The Duluth (Minnesota) Domestic Abuse Intervention Project, Praxis International (the technical assistance and training arm for the Office on Violence Against Women), and other research further expanded CARDV's thinking and improved our services.

One example of this is the use of the "cycle of violence" first identified in 1979 by Lenore Walker in *The Battered Woman*. Walker's model described a honeymoon period followed by a buildup of tension, a violent episode, apologies, another honeymoon period, and so on.

The Duluth Project, after working with batterer intervention programs, discovered that a crucial step was missing in the model. The "buildup of tension" stage did not just magically happen—abusers (and rapists) actually began fantasizing about committing abuse again. The addition of the "fantasizing" stage made the model more relevant, but still did not illustrate many survivors' experiences. By the early 2000s, based on Duluth's most current research, CARDV stopped using the model altogether.

Unfortunately, Walker's model is still widely referenced. A much more accurate tool and one to which all survivors can relate in some way is the Power and Control Wheel (see page 199) originally developed by Duluth in 1984. Physical and sexual violence form the rim of the wheel, the tactics an abuser uses to control his partner act as the spokes, and "power and control" is at the center— because sexual and domestic violence are fundamentally acts of power and control.

∽

From the movement's earliest days, the one question we could count on hearing each time we spoke out about violence against women was, "But what about the men?" The Straus and Gelles research in the late 1980s claiming that domestic violence was gender-neutral had influenced many, and a few could relate stories about a male friend who had been abused by a woman. Compounding the issue were the women who were convinced they had been just as abusive as the men who hurt them.

Though it wasn't until the year 2000 that we were able to offer shelter for males of all ages, CARDV has provided services for male survivors of sexual and domestic violence since our beginnings.

We deliberately do not use gender neutral language in our work because to do so would distort the reality of what is really happening.

The truth is, as Duluth's Domestic Abuse Intervention Project's research shows, eighty-six to ninety-seven percent of all criminal assaults (which include intimate partner violence incidences) are committed by men, and women are 3.5 times more likely to be killed than men in domestic homicides. In the instances where women are using violence against their male partners, they are primarily using it in response to the violence being used against them.

CARDV advocates look at patterns of behavior. Who is the one afraid in the relationship? What is the intent of the violence? Men will use violence to have power over and to control their victim's behavior. Women use violence most often as an effort to get the abuser to stop, or to defend herself. When women contacting CARDV say they have been just as violent as their male partners, advocates often ask: If he stopped being violent today, would you continue to use violence in the relationship? If you stopped using violence, would he continue? The survivors' answers are consistently "no" to the first question, and "yes" to the second.

As Jackson Katz, anti-sexist advocate and national speaker on gender violence prevention maintains: "While women's violence is wrong—if used for purposes other than self-defense—it is rarely part of a systematic pattern of power and control through force or the threat of force. On a wide range of issues from domestic violence and rape to stalking and sexual harassment, there is no symmetry between men's and women's violence against each other, no equivalence."

In the 1980s having a male volunteer doing direct service was such a rarity it merited a mention in the CARDV newsletter. Though few men sought attendance, The Oregon Coalition Against Sexual and Domestic Violence requested input from programs around the state before each annual conference on whether they should be allowed. Until the mid-1990s, the consensus was "no." Out of respect for the many advocates who had been sexually and physically abused by men, and wanting to create a safe space for all who attended, adult males were not welcome.

From the beginning, men served on CARDV's Board of Directors, participated in fundraising and community education, and helped keep our facilities in good repair. They have also made themselves available to male survivors requesting a male advocate. Men working with us have proven to be sensitive allies—acknowledging their male privilege and fully supporting CARDV's Mission and Principles of Unity.

Today men are expected participants in conferences and trainings. And men frequently attend CARDV's 40-hour advocacy training. Recognizing that the majority of callers are going to want to speak to a female, most choose not to answer the hotline, instead veering towards the shelter or legal advocacy programs.

The Men Ending Violence Coalition is another way men get involved. The CARDV-sponsored men's resource group works to educate the community about healthy masculinity and violence prevention.

In the early 2000s, CARDV's newsletter articles and letters to the editor adopted a different, more patient, tone. For the most part, the community got it. Occasional reminders of the facts now sufficed.

The general public still might not identify sexism as the root cause of sexual and domestic violence, but they do recognize the harm sexism causes women and girls and, in the end, the overall population. This is an enormous shift in awareness. Today, letters to the editor or posts to internet open forums denouncing sexism or criticizing the media's handling of sexual or domestic violence incidents are just as likely to come from individuals not connected to anti-violence work as they are from any of us.

CARDV helped bring about this cultural transformation.

Which is not to say that social change has been accomplished and we can cross it off our list. What it does mean is that the community has become a partner in our work. We are no longer on our own.

Once regarded with suspicion, our participation in advisory and working groups is now sought after. CARDV staff are currently or have in the past served on the Sexual Assault Response Team, Legal Aid Services Advisory Board, Vulnerable Adult Services Team, Oregon State University Sexual Assault Response and Prevention Alliance, Hispanic Advisory Council, Linn County Child Abuse Multidisciplinary Team, Benton County Affordable Housing Working Group, Milestones Advisory Board, Oregon State University Women's Center Advisory Board, Linn and Benton counties Family Violence Councils, DHS Domestic Violence Management Team, both Linn and Benton counties' Ten-Year Plans to Address Issues Surrounding Housing and Homelessness, Linn and Benton counties Commission on Children and Families, and Zonta, Soroptimists, Altrusa, and Rotary service groups.

Our participation in the Linn and Benton counties' Sexual Assault Response Teams, and our On-Scene Response and Lethality Assessment programs have allowed us to create partnerships with the district attorney offices, courts and law enforcement.

CARDV's leadership and expertise in the field has been

recognized throughout the state since the very beginning. CARDV board members testified at statewide hearings on domestic violence established by the governor. When founding staff members left CARDV, they went on to the Oregon Coalition Against Sexual and Domestic Violence to provide leadership and establish services across the state.

CARDV staff members have served on state-wide counsels, boards and committees, including: Crime Victims Services Division Advisory Board, Attorney General's Sexual Assault Task Force, Sexual Assault Nurse Examiners Commission, Oregon State Violence Against Women Act STOP Funds Advisory Board, State of Oregon DHS Domestic and Sexual Violence Fund Advisory Committee, and the Oregon Coalition Against Sexual and Domestic Violence Board.

From our unheralded beginning as a radical upstart challenging the status quo from the fringes of society, CARDV is now a respected community leader.

Part Two
Operations

Programs and Services

C ARDV services are available for all survivors of domestic and sexual violence regardless of ethnicity, religion, sexual orientation, gender identity, ability or age. Translation services are accessible 24/7. All CARDV services are free and confidential.

CURRENT PROGRAMS AND SERVICES

24-Hour Crisis and Support Line
January 14, 1977–Current

Callers can access all of CARDV's services through our 24-hour Crisis and Support Line. The phone number, 541-754-0110, is the same number one of CARDV's mother agencies, Corvallis Women Against Rape (CWAR), began answering January 14, 1977.

CWAR volunteers staffed the hotline between 7:00 p.m. Friday evening until 7:00 a.m. Sunday morning, utilizing an answering service to patch the calls through to their home phones. During the week, volunteers at Sunflower House (Community Outreach, Inc.) were trained to field calls. As the volunteer base grew, CWAR's hours were increased, until by 1980, the hotline was operational 24 hours a day, 7 days a week, 365 days a year.

Advocates answering the hotline provide crisis intervention; safety planning; safe shelter options; information about resources available in the community, including protection orders; one-on-one support and validation; and basic education about domestic violence/sexual assault/ stalking/sex trafficking dynamics so callers can make better informed choices about the situations they are experiencing. All calls are confidential.

It takes an enormous amount of courage for a survivor to pick up the phone, press in the number, and talk about what is happening to her. For many survivors, the first time they share the reality of what they are going through is with a CARDV advocate on the hotline.

The crisis and support line is available to survivors and their supporters, as well as to concerned community members. CARDV's many community partners utilize the hotline also—accessing our services on behalf of their clients, or brainstorming with us other possible courses of action and resources. During the fiscal year 2014–2015, we received 6,732 calls.

Confidential Safe Shelter
1979–Current

From its inception in November 1978, the Linn-Benton Association for the Prevention of Domestic Violence (CARDV's second mother agency) provided temporary safe shelter to domestic violence survivors. Volunteers transported the survivor and her children to Sunflower House (Community Outreach, Inc.), a rambling old yellow house at the south end of 9th Street in Corvallis. A Sunflower House volunteer would then drive her to the home of a community member—one of the safe houses within a small private home network. The survivor had just one to three days to decide what she was going to do next.

Today CARDV maintains two confidential safe shelters with a total of sixteen beds. When shelters are full clients can be housed in one of several motels in Linn and Benton counties. In cases when it is not safe for the survivor to stay in the area, we can provide transportation to another domestic violence agency in the state, or to a safe family member or friend.

The average shelter stay is fourteen days, but that varies depending upon the client's needs. It's not at all uncommon for a survivor to be in shelter for six weeks or longer.

Most shelter residents are starting their lives over again: finding housing, obtaining furniture and other household items, securing a job, establishing resources. Moving to a new place can be daunting for anyone—even when the relocation is carefully planned. But if the move is sudden, as when fleeing domestic violence, and the individual is afraid and in real danger of being found by her abuser, it can be overwhelming.

Both shelters are residential houses and provide a home-like environment. Each family is assigned their own bedroom, with kitchen, laundry facilities, and living areas shared. ADA and prescription companion animals are welcomed. If the resident has a disability that requires a caregiver, that person can accompany her. There is no age limit on the ages of the children, female or male, that the resident may bring with her to shelter.

Though domestic violence is overwhelmingly male to female violence, CARDV also receives calls from male survivors. With two shelters and motels available, we are able to accommodate male domestic violence survivors who need confidential safe shelter. CARDV accepted its first adult male survivor into shelter in 2000.

While in shelter, all the residents' needs are addressed: food, bedding, and toiletries are provided; clothing vouchers are supplied. Advocates meet with shelter residents daily to assess safety concerns and discuss options and resources. Sometimes survivors are forced to leave behind their jobs, or their children have to change schools because the threat of their abuser harming them is too great. Advocates help survivors enroll their children in new, safe schools and point them towards resources to find safe employment. If the resident wishes, an advocate will accompany her to DHS (Department of Human Services), legal, or other appointments. Childcare and transportation are provided when advocates are available.

During fiscal year 2014–2015 CARDV sheltered 115 women and 87 children for 3,345 bed nights.

Hospital Advocacy
1977–Current

CARDV advocates have been accompanying sexual assault survivors to the hospital since Corvallis Women Against Rape opened the hotline in January 1977. In those early years, two advocates typically responded to sexual assault calls. One advocate would be available to intervene on the survivor's behalf if she did not wish to report or speak to law enforcement, leaving the other free to focus all her attention on the survivor herself. Frequently advocates were placed in the position of having to explain the workings of the rape kit to a nurse or doctor unfamiliar with forensic evidence collection.

When a sexual assault survivor goes to the hospital today, her experience will be very different. The CARDV advocate is but one component of the Sexual Assault Response Team (SART). A specially trained Sexual Assault Nurse Examiner will examine the survivor and, if the survivor chooses, perform the sexual assault forensic evidence collection. At every point during the exam, the survivor will be reminded of her options. Law enforcement will be available if she chooses to report. If she is unsure about reporting, she has the option of doing an "anonymous" kit—in which evidence will be collected and stored by the appropriate law enforcement agency for up to six months. The Sexual Assault Victim's Emergency Fund will pay for the medical exam and/or the forensic kit (when performed within 84 hours of the assault) whether the survivor reports to law enforcement or not.

CARDV advocates respond to domestic violence calls as well. We meet survivors at the emergency department and occasionally we are called to talk with a patient who discloses to hospital staff that she isn't safe to return home.

In addition to Student Health Services at Oregon State University, advocates respond to all three hospitals in Linn and Benton counties 24/7.

Legal Advocacy
1977–Current

From the first days of the hotline, CARDV has helped survivors navigate the often intimidating court system. At a caller's request, advocates assisted in filling out protection orders and accompanied the caller to restraining order or stalking order hearings, contested hearings, and other court proceedings relating to domestic and sexual violence.

In the mid-1990s the program was formalized and today advocates are in both Linn and Benton County courthouses every day to offer assistance to petitioners. Advocates attend the hearings and provide safety planning, information, and support to the survivors. For many of the petitioners, it is their first contact with CARDV. During the fiscal year 2014–2015, the Legal Advocacy Program served more than 900 individuals.

Volunteer Program and Advocacy Training
1977–Current

Both of CARDV's mother agencies were founded and run by volunteers. The Linn-Benton Association for the Prevention of Domestic Violence hired a part-time administrative assistant six months after its incorporation, leaving much of both client and administrative services dependent upon volunteers. The same was true of the Rape Crisis Center: a director and a part-time CETA (Comprehensive Employment and Training Act) employee provided services Monday through Friday 8:00 a.m. to 5:00 p.m., with volunteers covering nights and weekends.

Today, paid staff administer CARDV services around the clock, but volunteers continue to play a crucial role in every aspect of the agency. The board of directors is an all-volunteer board, responsible for CARDV's fiscal health and supervision of the executive director. We couldn't hold any of our fund-raising events, including the popular Spaghetti Dinner, the Safe Families Breakfast, or the Mother's Day 5K Run and Fun Walk for Safe Families, if it weren't for the hundreds of volunteers who donate their time. Volunteers assist us with administrative tasks, staffing the reception desk at the Advocacy Center, and organizing donations. Families and service organizations organize wish drives for CARDV, supplying our clients with toiletries and other basic necessities.

CARDV holds two 40-hour advocacy trainings a year for those who wish to work directly with survivors of domestic and sexual violence, stalking, or sex trafficking. After successful completion of the training and a minimum of an additional ten hours of job-shadowing, volunteers can answer the 24-hour crisis hotline, participate in the Hospital and Legal Advocacy programs, or take part in the Shelter Volunteer Program.

CARDV's 40-hour advocacy training adheres to the requirements adopted by the State of Oregon Department of Human Services Domestic and Sexual Violence Advisory Committee. Additionally, further trainings are held throughout the year so that all staff and volunteers who work directly with clients have the most up-to-date information available.

Support Groups
Pre-1980–Current

Beginning in the early 1980's and continuing through most of the 1990s, the demand for support groups was so high it seemed CARDV couldn't offer enough. CARDV facilitated weekly domestic violence and sexual assault support groups in Corvallis, Albany, Lebanon, and Sweet Home. A teen dating violence group met in Corvallis. Additionally, beginning in 1982, an adult incest survivors support group was offered periodically, as well as one for non-offending partners of survivors. In the late 1980s a group was held for survivors who were lesbians, and in 2005 a domestic violence support group was conducted for Spanish speakers.

Sometime in the early 2000s survivors' needs shifted.

Rather than attending groups, more and more survivors requested one-on-one meetings.

Today support groups are organized whenever several survivors express an interest and are held primarily in Corvallis and Albany. Different topics are the focal points of discussion each week, including: safety planning, healthy relationships, boundaries, self-care, and healthy sexual intimacy.

Winter Holiday Program
Late 1980s–Current

CARDV's Winter Holiday Program began in an Adopt-a-Family style. Community members and groups adopted a CARDV family and provided all the trimmings: wrapped presents and sometimes a decorated tree and the fixings for a holiday dinner.

Wanting to give parents an opportunity to have a more active role in their children's holiday, in 2000 the program began evolving into the CARDV Holiday Open House. Community members donate gifts for the program, and the night before the event, volunteers arrange the toys, clothing, books, art supplies, and other items, turning CARDV's office into a festive "store."

Clients who have worked with CARDV during the previous year are invited to shop for free. Transportation and childcare are provided. After shopping, parents wrap presents at the gift wrap station and share the happenings in their lives with the advocates and other clients. Everyone gets their fill of cider, freshly baked cookies, and chocolate.

Probably the most memorable Open House was in 2007

after a storm the night before knocked the top half of our giant spruce onto the roof of the Blake House, cutting off the power. With the sump pump incapacitated, the basement, where the children's room was housed at the time, filled with more than six inches of ground water.

Fortunately, holiday gifts had been stored in the attic. Advocates grabbed flashlights and set up the holiday "store," an advocate's office was turned into childcare space, and the Open House began right on schedule. That year forty-four families shopped for their ninety-one children.

Lawyer Referral Program
1995–Current

Most CARDV clients do not have the means to secure an attorney and if the perpetrator has representation, the survivor is at greater risk of having her protection order overturned; or in cases involving custody, losing her children. Throughout the 1980s and 1990s, depending upon their limited resources, Legal Aid designated a number of referrals each year for our clients. But often Legal Aid was not an option for the survivor.

Today, a number of attorneys offer their services pro bono through CARDV's Lawyer Referral Program, started as an AmeriCorps project in 1995. In addition, Legal Aid schedules one morning every two weeks to meet our clients at CARDV's Advocacy Center.

Court Watch
Mid-1990s–Intermittent

The Court Watch program was designed to improve the legal justice system process for survivors of stalking, and domestic and sexual violence by increasing communication between clients, advocates, and judges. Advocates attending protective order hearings record outcomes of the hearings on a Court Watch form, as well as comments made by the judges to the petitioners. Periodically CARDV presents reports to the presiding judges of both counties detailing concerns as well as appreciation. Judges have been extremely receptive to our feedback, Benton County even going so far as to change the times protective order hearings were held so that CARDV advocates could be on hand daily to assist petitioners.

Pet Boarding
2000–Current

Animals provide a great deal of emotional support, which can be a lifeline to someone living in violence. Numerous studies show there is an extremely high correlation between animal abuse and domestic violence—with as many as 71 percent of women entering domestic violence shelters around the country reporting their abuser had either injured or killed the family pet. It is therefore not surprising that many women are unable to leave their abusive situation for fear of what will happen to their beloved animal.

Begun as an AmeriCorps project, CARDV's Pet Boarding Program provides pets with safe shelter until the resident can secure permanent housing. Heartland Humane Society boards most of our clients' pets, and in the rare cases they are unable to, we have a number of local vets who have agreed to assist.

Women's Independence Scholarship Program, Inc.
2000–Current

Created by The Sunshine Lady Foundation, Women's Independence Scholarship Program was founded in 1999 in Wilmington, North Carolina by Doris Buffett. The program provides scholarships to women survivors of intimate partner abuse who wish to obtain a college degree.

CARDV is able to sponsor a limited number of clients at a time for the program and several have gone on to obtain not only two- or four-year college degrees, but also advanced degrees.

The Sunshine Lady Foundation is one of those rare foundations that truly understands the obstacles women face when leaving domestic violence. The applicant needs to be safe from her former abusive partner and maintain close contact with her domestic violence advocate/sponsor to the program. In addition to tuition, books and fees which are paid directly to the school, the program will often cover such necessary expenses as childcare, utilities, transportation, etc.

CARDV assists the client with budgeting and record-keeping, and disburses the funds for the duration of the scholarship.

Shelter Volunteer Program
2003–Current

Also originally an AmeriCorps project, the Shelter Volunteer Program is a flexible program designed to accommodate the needs of individual shelter residents. Volunteers participating in the program might find themselves helping a resident figure out how to read the Corvallis Transit System's bus map and maybe even riding the bus with her the first time. Most importantly, the volunteers are available to spend time with the children.

Shelter volunteers provide that family support that is necessary during this time when residents and their children are undergoing so much transition in their lives. Residents appreciate the extra help between the hours of six and eight in the evening, when they are busy cooking dinner or preparing for bedtimes. And they especially welcome an opportunity to have some time to themselves—to shower, take a nap, or even to go to the grocery.

Many survivors have never been allowed to make decisions or move about on their own before leaving their abusers. Having an advocate available in shelter allows the survivor the time to recognize her own strengths and skills, and to get help when she needs it.

On Scene Response
2005–Current

In 2005, the Linn County District Attorney's office received a two-year grant from the Office on Violence Against Women (VAWA) to restructure the way domestic violence cases were addressed. A part-time judge was hired through the grant, and the newly created Domestic Violence Court expedited the handling of domestic violence cases from the time of arrest, through arraignment, and to trial. Previously, perpetrators had often been released shortly after their arrest and then returned to court for their arraignment. Domestic Violence Court allowed for domestic violence cases to be "fast tracked" through the system, cutting down on offenders being released from jail early. Additionally, offenders were required to report to court monthly to monitor their compliance with sentencing requirements.

The grant, which CARDV co-wrote with the District Attorney's Office, also provided for two full-time crisis response advocates. When Linn County law enforcement responded to a domestic violence incident and arrested the abusive partner, the officer or deputy called CARDV.

Two crisis response advocates were made available 24/7 to respond to the home after an arrest was made. In the immediate aftermath of the crisis, advocates provided safety planning and talked with the survivor about all the services available for her. Her children had most likely witnessed the abuse and advocates could sit with them while she made phone calls or gathered up her belongings to leave the home. If the survivor wished, the advocates could assist her with completing a restraining order packet and arrange for transportation to court. Shelter was offered as an option, or if the survivor had another safe place in mind, transportation. The first year of the grant, CARDV advocates drove over 25,000 miles for client-related services.

Many survivors stay in contact with CARDV advocates long after that initial contact: accessing legal advocacy and court hearing information, and addressing housing, education, employment, and other needs.

Even though the grant was not renewed after 2009 and Domestic Violence Court is no longer held independently, the grant had a permanent impact in how domestic violence is addressed in Linn County. Law enforcement continues to call CARDV for on-scene response, and the relationships formed with law enforcement and the District Attorney's Office during the grant period created a greater safety net for survivors.

Address Confidentiality Program
2006–Current

CARDV advocates are all certified application assistants for the Address Confidentiality Program. Established and administered by the Department of Justice, Criminal Justice Division, the Address Confidentiality Program enables survivors of domestic violence, sexual assault, stalking, or human trafficking to protect their physical address from the individuals who have harmed them. The Post Office box number supplied to program participants can be used anywhere a physical address is traditionally required— even on a driver's license or voter's registration.

This program has been life saving for survivors whose

abusers continue to stalk them after they leave. Technology has made it far too easy for perpetrators to locate their victims. A Post Office box through the Address Confidentiality Program helps keep her location concealed.

Lethality Assessment Program
2009–Current

In 2009 CARDV was selected as one of five sites nationally to be trained in the use of a Lethality Screening Tool and Protocol for first responders to incidents of domestic violence. In order to take part in this program, it was necessary for all eight law enforcement agencies in our service area to agree to participate. And without hesitation they signed on: Albany Police Department, Lebanon Police Department, Sweet Home Police Department, Linn County Sheriff's Office, Corvallis Police Department, Philomath Police Department, Benton County Sheriff's Office, and Oregon State Police.

The protocol, developed by the Maryland Network Against Domestic Violence in partnership with researchers from John Hopkins University, profoundly reduces the number of homicides of adult and child victims of domestic violence. In counties where the protocol has been in place over time and used consistently, domestic violence homicides have ended.

Law enforcement responding to an incident of domestic violence utilize an eleven-question lethality screen that predicts danger and lethality. The screen, developed by Dr. Jacquelyn Campbell from John Hopkins University, is a proactive approach: research showed that only 4 percent of intimate partner murder victims had ever accessed domestic violence services.

After administering the screen, law enforcement calls CARDV. If an arrest has been made and it is safe to do so, the advocate can meet with the survivor on-scene. If no arrest has been made, the advocate speaks with the survivor on the officer or deputy's phone to safety plan, provide information about services available, and set up a time to meet in person. As in the On-Scene Response program, many survivors stay in touch with advocates long after that initial contact.

Supportive Housing
2012–Current

CARDV began imagining a supportive housing program (or "transitional housing" as it was called in those days) even before we finished moving furniture into our first shelter in 1982.

A few weeks in a confidential safe shelter just isn't long enough to regain all one loses when living with a violent partner. The very nature of intimate partner violence erodes the victim's confidence and sense of self-worth. She is probably struggling with post-traumatic stress and depression. It may be a long time before she feels secure again. As financial abuse is a common tactic used in domestic violence, she most likely doesn't have any monetary resources. And if she has a credit history, all too often it has been ruined by her abuser.

Additionally, it is difficult to obtain safe affordable housing in Benton and Linn counties. Sometimes when survivors cannot find a place to live and have no other resources, their only option is to return to their abusers.

Over the years, we were able to periodically partner with an agency offering temporary transitional housing, and provided case management and support for the domestic violence survivors. But these programs were sporadic, and often the housing units were spread throughout the community making transportation a challenge.

In 2002 CARDV and Willamette Neighborhood Housing began exploring the idea of a joint affordable housing project. The resulting development, Alexander Court, opened in May 2012, with ten apartments in the 24-unit complex designated for domestic violence survivors.

The Advocacy Center, CARDV's public face in the community, is located in the complex, providing case management to residents as well as hosting classes and events for the community.

CARDV's program offers a continuum of services, based on individual clients' needs, to provide survivors with the necessary skills to feel more confident in their ability to become self-sufficient.

Past Programs

Children's Program
1982–2008

The Children's Program was overseen by the children's coordinator. She met individually with each mom and child coming into shelter and focused on assisting moms with parenting concerns. Arts, crafts, and play groups were offered when the shelter population warranted.

Now all advocates work with the children. With so many good resources in the community available, advocates make parenting referrals to the experts if the mother deems it necessary.

CARDV has always believed that if the mother is safe she will be able to keep her children safe. Services are therefore primarily focused on the survivor. Advocates can watch the children while she has an appointment, or are available for respite childcare when she needs to take some time for herself.

The homelike atmosphere of the shelters gives children a safe place to reconnect with their mothers and establish normalcy. Advocates provide children with kind, consistent attention which helps them feel they are welcomed and belong.

Counseling Program
Late 1980s–Approximately 2002

Through the 1980s and early 1990s CARDV contracted with several different therapists to offer counseling for survivors of domestic and sexual violence, as well as 12-week closed therapy groups for adults molested as children.

From 1992 to 1997 CARDV had a full-time counselor on staff as part of the Women In Transition Project, our joint project with Community Outreach, Inc. In addition to the program participants, the counselor met with shelter residents and our other clients. Then in 1998 a one-year grant paid for a 22-hour a week counselor who provided counseling for shelter residents and survivors in the community.

For the next three years, until 2002, retired counselors volunteering their services and interns from the counseling program at Oregon State University met with CARDV clients.

Today, CARDV focuses on crisis intervention, advocacy, and transitional services rather than an on-going counseling program. Advocates assist clients in choosing a therapist who will best suit their needs by helping them establish interview questions to ask. A suitable counselor will have a thorough understanding of the dynamics of domestic and sexual violence and understand how vital safety planning is for the client.

Parent Effectiveness Training
Early 1990s

In the early 1990s, the most sought-after shelter shift for staff and volunteers was Tuesday evening, 5:30 p.m. to 9:00 p.m. That was the night the CARDV volunteer and certified Parent Effectiveness Training instructor came to the shelter to facilitate a weekly parent support group.

Parent Effectiveness Training, developed by Dr. Thomas Gordon in 1962, taught skills for creating a collaborative relationship between the parent and the child. Through active listening and I-message exercises, parents practiced no-lose conflict resolution steps designed to resolve conflicts in such a way that both the parent and the child got their needs met.

Former shelter residents joined current residents for the group. After a potluck supper, the children participated in the arts and crafts and games lead by volunteers in the children's room. As staff and volunteers cleaned the kitchen, clients gathered around the big oak dining table as the instructor set up her flip chart outlining the values and principles of the program.

Rarely did she get through more than two pages before moms were sharing experiences and ideas. The former residents brought understanding and encouragement to current residents and before the evening was over, new friendships were formed.

Nurturing Program
October 1995–June 1996

CARDV's children's program coordinator, with the assistance of twenty-two volunteers, coordinated the Nurturing Program, developed by Family Development Resources, Inc.

Non-offending parents referred by partner agencies joined former shelter residents for the twelve-week Nurturing Program sessions. Sessions were provided once a week in both Linn and Benton counties.

Local restaurants provided dinner. After families ate together, they met with their individual groups: one for parents, one for children ages zero to three, children ages four to eight, and children ages nine to twelve. The same concepts were addressed during each group: for example, as parents learned how to understand and respond to their children's feelings, their children were learning how to express their feelings.

Up to ten families attended each of the five twelve-week sessions, with over one hundred adults and children participating.

The Nurturing Program proved far too big for one agency to support and the following year several non-profits and community members assumed responsibility for the program.

AmeriCorps
1995–2004

Established during President Clinton's Administration, AmeriCorps was patterned after VISTA (Volunteers In Service to America), established in 1963, and CETA (Comprehensive Employment and Training Act) created in 1973: addressing local community problems with Federal support. VISTA and CETA programs made it possible for early domestic violence and sexual assault programs, including CARDV, to employ paid staff.

In 1995 the Oregon Coalition Against Domestic and Sexual Violence partnered with Oregon Legal Services to create the AmeriCorps project, "The Community Partnership to Stop Violence Against Women." The project provided for six attorneys based at Legal Aid offices, and fifteen advocates placed at selected domestic violence and sexual assault programs. The assignments lasted for eighteen months. An advocate was appointed to CARDV the first year of the project and we continued to participate until 2004.

Each AmeriCorps member, under the guidance of CARDV, designed and implemented her own project, with the objective that the project continue after her appointment was completed. Some of the projects included: the Attorney Referral Program, the Pet Boarding Program, the Shelter Volunteer Program, and the establishment of an Albany outreach office.

Substance Abuse Program
2000–2001

A one-year special projects grant through United Way Benton County added an eight-hour a week Drug and Alcohol Certified Counselor to CARDV's staff. The counselor met with new shelter residents to do assessments when appropriate and make referrals to treatment programs. Classes on alcohol and other drugs were offered to current and former shelter residents.

Substance abuse does not cause domestic violence, but studies indicate high rates of use among perpetrators during incidents of abuse. Also, women living in domestic violence will sometimes turn to substances as a means to cope with the violence. Women dealing with addiction issues are especially vulnerable. Few domestic violence or homeless shelters will accept anyone unless they have been clean and sober for at least five days—which can be a huge barrier for many survivors, and may even be life-threatening.

Although CARDV's Substance Abuse Program was short lived, the impact on our services was permanent. We make every effort to screen clients *into* shelter rather than screening them *out*: if necessary placing the survivor in a motel for a night or two before bringing into shelter.

VOCA Project Civil Legal Program
2000–2004

A four-year project grant from the Victims of Crime Act allowed CARDV to contract with Legal Aid Services of Oregon for a half-time attorney to staff family law cases involving domestic and sexual violence. In addition to offering technical assistance and training to CARDV advocates, the Legal Aid attorney provided CARDV's clients with much-needed representation with contested restraining orders, stalking orders, divorce and custody cases.

Albany Emergency Shelter Program
2014–2015

CARDV received a Community Development Block Grant (CDBG) from the City of Albany for a limited shelter program the first year Albany's population topped 50,000 and became eligible to administer the Federal grant funds.

Since both CARDV's existing shelters were purchased with City of Corvallis Community Development Block Grant funds, they are located in Corvallis. For many survivors living in Albany, coming to Corvallis for shelter is a hardship: interrupting their work or schooling, or cutting them off from family and friends they depend upon for support. More than half of CARDV's shelter residents come from Linn County. The Albany grant funds made it possible for these survivors to stay in a motel in Albany, if it was safe for them to do so.

The grant was not continued for a second year, but it gave CARDV the opportunity to develop relationships with the motels in Albany. Frequently Corvallis residents are safer in Albany, just as all too often Albany residents are safer in Corvallis. Having Albany motels as an option gives advocates more flexibility when safety planning with survivors.

Funding

Being a grassroots organization, CARDV's first funding relied entirely on fundraising efforts and private donations. Predictable and dependable funding is of vital importance in order to provide consistent services for survivors.

CARDV's annual budget for fiscal year 2015–2016 was $1,029,294. Of that amount, 73 percent came in the form of "restricted" funds—meaning, from grants dictating how the funds can be used. This figure also includes the occasional request from a private donor who asks that their donation be used in a specific way, such as toys for the shelter, or gifts for the Winter Holiday Program.

That leaves 27 percent in "unrestricted" funds—general funds to cover operating expenses and everything else that isn't grant funded. This includes all utilities and maintenance on CARDV's two shelters, administrative office, and Advocacy Center; bus tickets when survivors have to relocate for their safety; shelter food, towels, bedding and toiletries for residents; paying for motel nights when the shelters are full. CARDV's biggest office expense is telephone and internet—$17,000 budgeted for 2015–2016. There are never enough unrestricted funds to cover everything: for example, during fiscal year 2013–2014 repairs and maintenance topped $16,000, which included $4,500 for an emergency sewer line replacement.

PRIVATE FOUNDATIONS AND DONORS
1977–Current

The community has responded to CARDV's needs with extraordinary generosity. Donors and private foundations have helped CARDV pay for such diverse needs as an alarm system for one of the shelters; a two-year grant for a development director; sweat pants and T-shirts for our hospital-response bags; and the building of our Advocacy Center. Most private foundations are project-driven with a competitive grant application process, but every year CARDV receives unexpected generous checks from local private foundations.

During fiscal year 2014–2015, CARDV received $64,737 from private foundations. Donors contributed $176,215 through monthly donations, CARDV's Holiday Letter, newsletter, community events, and United Way workplace contributions.

COMMUNITY DEVELOPMENT BLOCK GRANTS (CDBG)
1981–as applied for

Community Development Block Grants are federal funds available to communities with populations of 50,000 larger. CARDV's first confidential shelter, now serving as our publically accessible administrative office, was purchased through a competitive Corvallis Community Development Block Grant in 1981. In 2003, we purchased a second shelter, also through a Block Grant. The property for our Advocacy Center which was completed in April, 2012 was a Corvallis Block Grant as well.

In addition, CARDV has also undergone numerous facility rehabilitation projects funded through the Corvallis competitive grants, including: widening the driveway at our administrative office; replacing a water-damaged kitchen floor; installing energy efficient vinyl windows; bringing wheelchair ramps up to code; replacing exterior siding; upgrading our security alarm systems; and many other repairs and upgrades.

In 2014, the first year the City of Albany became eligible for Community Development Block Grant funds, CARDV was able to establish an Emergency Shelter Program in Albany utilizing Albany motels.

MARRIAGE LICENSE TAX
1982-Current

In 1982 CARDV received $18,060 from the State of Oregon Marriage License Tax administered through Children's Services Division (now Department of Human Services). This was the first state funding specifically to address domestic and sexual violence and the legislature had not passed the bill without a fight.

The bill, introduced at the request of the Oregon Coalition Against Domestic and Sexual Violence, called for a $10 increase in the marriage license tax with the monies being used to set up a statewide child and family abuse hotline and to provide funding for shelters and safe houses across the state. The intent was to stabilize existing programs and to aid underserved areas of Oregon.

The bill was highly controversial and ridiculed by many. A conservative legislator nearly derailed the bill when he pointed out that its passage might be suggesting that marriage had something to do with domestic violence.

The Oregon Coalition Against Domestic and Sexual Violence and the Women's Rights Coalition led the grass-roots lobbying effort. Women from domestic violence programs all over the state came to Salem to testify on behalf of the bill. Supporters who couldn't get to Salem participated in a prodigious letter writing campaign.

After the bill was passed and the money committed, the Oregon Coalition Against Domestic and Sexual Violence and the programs lobbied Children's Services Division to set up a committee with representatives from domestic violence programs to oversee the fund. The fear was that the money would be used for competitively selected projects and the Coalition wanted to ensure that services were funded all over the state. The Domestic and Sexual Violence Fund Advisory Committee was established and written into the statute. Over the years several CARDV staff members have served on the statewide committee.

During fiscal year 2015–2016, CARDV received $26,832 in unrestricted funds from the Marriage License Tax.

United Way—Linn and Benton Counties
1982–Current

Both United Ways in Linn and Benton counties have provided funding to CARDV since 1982. During fiscal year 2015–2016, Benton County United Way combined with the City of Corvallis helped fund CARDV's Crisis Response with $12,940. Linn County's $8,500 contributed towards CARDV's shelter program and general advocacy.

FEMA
1984–Current

CARDV became eligible for FEMA funds from Linn and Benton counties in 1984. FEMA assists with CARDV's shelter budget by reimbursing $12.50 per bed-night up to $5,000 per year, which equates to 400 bed-nights. During fiscal year 2014–2015, CARDV had a total of 3,345 bed-nights.

FAMILY VIOLENCE PREVENTION AND SERVICES ACT (FVPSA)
1985–Current

The Family Violence Prevention and Services Act, passed in 1984, was the first federal funding for domestic violence crisis lines, emergency shelters, and related services.

In 1980, when debates began for the legislation, one senator stated, "I think it would be distinctly wrong for the federal government to get involved in this very delicate matter, which goes right to the heart of the American family, which is the basis of society." He went on to say, "I fear the grantees are opposed to traditional families... The funding would sustain, quote homes for battered women, unquote. What kind of values and ideas would these homes advise? The federal government should not fund missionaries who would war on the traditional family or local values." Another senator said, "I cannot support legislation which gives every indication of supporting activities which can only undermine the ability of many families to resolve their problems while preserving their unity."

CARDV advocates and our supporters embarked upon a relentless letter writing campaign in which we educated our senators and representatives about the dynamics of domestic violence, strongly urging them to vote in favor of the legislation. The National Coalition Against Domestic Violence, domestic violence and sexual assault programs, and women's groups from across the country worked long and hard to get the act passed.

During fiscal year 2015–2016, CARDV received $60,072 in unrestricted funds from the Family Violence Prevention and Services Act.

Victims of Crime Act (VOCA)
1986–Current

Federal passage of the Victims of Crime Act was authorized in 1984, with funds becoming available to domestic violence and sexual assault programs in 1986. The fund was created by Congress to provide federal support to state and local programs assisting victims of crime. Funds are acquired from fines and penalties received from offenders at the federal level—not taxpayer revenue.

CARDV participated in a letter writing campaign with programs across the state urging David Frohnmayer, Oregon's Attorney General at the time, to ensure the $490,000 Oregon was slated to receive would be divided among the thirty-three domestic violence and sexual assault programs.

Nationally, more than 3.8 million crime victims are served each year by 4,400 agencies from all fifty-six states and territories dependent upon Victims of Crime Act assistance grants. During the fiscal year 2015–2016, CARDV received $233,028 in Victims of Crime Act funds. The funds help subsidize CARDV's crisis hotline, Legal Advocacy Program, Volunteer Program, and shelter services. CARDV is required to make a 25 percent match, which is accomplished through volunteer hours and private donations.

OREGON TAX RETURN CHECK-OFF OPTION
1992–Current

Oregon Coalition Against Domestic and Sexual Violence launched an Oregon tax return check-off campaign, "Stop Domestic and Sexual Violence" in 1991. The charitable check-off had to raise $100,000 during the initial two-year tax return period for 1991 and 1992, for the option to remain. CARDV joined programs from all over the state and wrote letters to newspaper editors, and encouraged friends, family, co-workers, neighbors, and community members to donate a portion of their state refund to "Stop Domestic and Sexual Violence."

Proceeds from the state tax return continue to be distributed by the Coalition to domestic violence and sexual assault programs throughout the state. The 2014 check-off netted CARDV $1,444 in unrestricted funds.

VIOLENCE AGAINST WOMEN ACT (VAWA)
1995–Current

In 1994 President Clinton signed the Violence Against Women Act as part of the Violent Crime Control and Law Enforcement Act. Vice President Joseph Biden, then a senator, initiated this landmark legislation in 1990 by submitting a proposal to Congress addressing the issue of violence against women.

When the bill passed in 1994, it was the first comprehensive federal legislation designed to end violence against women. It was also a victory for domestic violence and sexual assault programs, state coalitions, and women's groups across the country who lobbied hard for its passage.

The Violence Against Women Act provides grants to strengthen law enforcement, prosecution, and services to victims of domestic violence, sexual assault and stalking. During fiscal year 2015–2016 CARDV received $20,995 to help fund shelter services.

CRIMINAL FINE ASSESSMENT ACCOUNT FUND (CFAA)

1996–Current (Criminal Fine Assessment Account Fund—Domestic Violence)
2000–Current (Criminal Fine Assessment Account Fund—Sexual Assault)

In 1983 the Oregon Legislature authorized the Oregon Department of Justice, Crime Victims' Assistance Section (now Crime Victims' Services Division) to disburse a portion of the monies from the Criminal Fine and Assessment Account to counties and cities where district attorney offices were maintaining comprehensive victims' assistance programs.

The Oregon Legislature included the Domestic Violence Fund as one of the recipients to receive a percentage of the funds in 1995. In 1999 the Legislature authorized disbursements to the Sexual Assault Fund.

During fiscal year 2015–2016, CARDV received $64,224 in Domestic Violence funds (with a 25 percent match from CARDV) and $13,356 in Sexual Assault funds. The funds are unrestricted, but must be used for domestic violence and sexual assault services.

OREGON DOMESTIC AND SEXUAL VIOLENCE SERVICES FUND (ODSVS)
2002–Current

In 2001 the Alliance Against Violence Against Women successfully lobbied the Oregon Legislature to create the Oregon Domestic and Sexual Violence Services Fund—the first General Fund money dedicated to domestic violence and sexual assault.

During fiscal year 2015–2016, CARDV's sexual assault response program was partially funded through $57,318 in sexual assault restricted funds. CARDV also received $103,390 in domestic violence unrestricted funds.

Fundraising

Fundraising generates those unrestricted funds so critical to CARDV's operating expenses and services that aren't grant funded. Being a grassroots organization, all of CARDV's original funding came from fundraising and private donations.

The financial return of fundraising endeavors has to be weighed against the popularity of the event as well as the amount of staff time the event takes to organize. A Meyer Memorial Trust grant in 2005 funded CARDV's first development director, a position which was later restructured as our communications and events director. During fiscal year 2015–2016, the Oregon Community Foundation awarded CARDV a grant to fund a development director who, together with our communications and events director, achieves the growth and outreach goals for CARDV. Having individuals dedicated to overseeing CARDV's development and fundraising efforts, frees advocates to focus on survivor needs.

CURRENT FUNDRAISING EVENTS

Community Sponsored Events
1979–Current

CARDV has been the recipient of the generosity of community members and organizations since CARDV's earliest days. Performers hold concerts on our behalf, restaurants and stores donate a portion of their day's receipts. Sororities, community groups and service organizations host auctions, raffles, wish list drives, and golf tournaments; and a local tattoo shop once offered a month-long "get a tattoo for CARDV" promotion.

In 2014, the Corvallis Rotary Half Marathon brought CARDV $6,096; and Many Hands Trading wrote us a check for $5,264 from their Day of Caring event. The community event, MockRock, organized by Oregon State University's Kappa Delta Sorority netted CARDV $29,021 in 2015.

Probably the most unusual donation came in 1983 when Benton County Judge Henry Dickerson ordered a man convicted of a sex offense to give $1,200 to CARDV as part of his fine.

Spaghetti Dinner
1979–1999, 2002–Current

CARDV's oldest and longest running fundraiser is the popular Spaghetti Dinner. Originally billed as the "All You Can Eat Spaghetti Dinner," the event was held at a Corvallis church, with staff and volunteers doing the cooking, serving, and cleaning up. For the 1984 dinner, tickets were $4 for adults, and $3 for children and those over the age of 65. It was declared a financial success with a profit of $875. Later, Mazzi's, a local Italian food restaurant, took on the dinner for us and supplied the food and the cooks. They continued the tradition until they relocated their restaurant to Eugene.

In 1999, CARDV determined the fundraiser had become too labor-intensive for staff to maintain and discontinued the event. One of CARDV's former board members declared the spaghetti dinner was as important to the community as it was to CARDV, and contacted other former board members who agreed with her. The event has been volunteer-run since 2002.

The Spaghetti Dinner *is* important to the community. A number of the participants started attending the dinner with their parents when they were children and are now bringing their own children. Each year more than 200 people pack into a Corvallis meeting hall to connect with old friends and feast on spaghetti.

Holiday Letter
1985–Current

CARDV's first Holiday Letter, titled "A Chance to be a Friend," didn't make it out to supporters until April of 1985. My Sister's Place, the Lincoln County domestic violence program, had done a similar fundraiser, and CARDV hoped to bring in at least $1,000. There's no record of the letter's earnings from that year, but in 2015 our supporters mailed us $28,342 in response to the Holiday Letter.

Mother's Day Fun Run for Safe Families
2003–Current

An early forerunner of CARDV's Fun Run was the 1981 Walk-a-Thon, a one-time event that netted $1,000. Seventeen walkers and thirty-two runners participated.

Today's event, the Mother's Day Fun Run for Safe Families, consists of a 5K run, a 2-mile walk, and a kids dash. The festivities include live music, raffle ticket prize drawings, safety fair, bubble table for the kids, and a talking fire hydrant. McGruff the Crime Dog is on hand and Oregon State University's Benny Beaver and Linn-Benton Community College's Rocky the Roadrunner cheer the runners and walkers on.

More than 100 volunteers help with the event: obtaining and sorting raffle prizes; setting up outdoor canopies for information tables; handing out T-shirts and participant numbers; marking the courses; directing traffic; doling out water, oranges and bananas. Teams compete to see who can recruit the most members, and from the looks of many of them, the funniest hats.

In 2015, 349 entrants participated and netted CARDV $17,166.

Safe Families Breakfast
2007–Current

The Safe Families Breakfast has thus far been CARDV's most successful fundraising endeavor. Held at the CH2M Hill Alumni Center, eight attendees fill each of the thirty to forty tables draped with crisp white tablecloths. The guests, each of whom was invited by their table captain, are served a continental breakfast. Brief welcoming speeches from CARDV's board chair and executive director introduce the event, followed by a five-minute video highlighting CARDV's role in the community. The most impactful portion of the program, for CARDV staff as well as the attendees, is when a survivor speaks, giving testimony as to how significant CARDV's services have been to her life. A community member closes the event by asking for donations and pledges.

The event itself lasts for one hour, though many attendees arrive early and stay late to drink coffee and visit with friends and CARDV staff.

In 2015, the Safe Families Breakfast netted CARDV $50,300.

PAST FUNDRAISING EVENTS

Corvallis Fall Festival
Tostada booth 1982–1991
Corn booth 1992–1999

CARDV was a fixture at the Corvallis Fall Festival food court for eighteen years, first with tostadas and later with corn on the cob. Both ventures proved to be extremely labor-intensive. When the farmer who had supplied the corn elected to grow different crops, it seemed like a good time for us to step away from food service and stick to spaghetti once a year.

Phone-a-Thon
1988–2001 Phone-a-Thon
2002–2006 Campaign for Hope

Board members, staff, and volunteers spent two weeks' worth of evenings dialing for donations for thirteen years before CARDV decided cold-calling possible donors wasn't the best use of anyone's time. We contracted with a community member who conducted "Campaign for Hope" for the next five years. The phone campaign increased our donor base considerably. Still, CARDV wasn't entirely comfortable with the impersonal mass calling approach and discontinued the event. Now staff and board members stay in touch with our supporters through letters and personal phone calls.

In One Place
1994–2001

CARDV, along with numerous other non-profits, participated in the upscale winter holiday boutique, In One Place.
Open through November and December, the store raised
funds for local children's programs. Prior to the event a
Corvallis retailer provided catalogues featuring a wide
array of products for agencies to choose from, and advocates voted for their favorites which would carry CARDV's
name on the tags. Advocates and volunteers filled in at the
store between their hotline and shelter shifts.

Twice Upon a Time
2003–2006

CARDV joined other local non-profits to support a community member in the opening of a resale shop, Twice Upon
a Time, in downtown Corvallis. Non-profit volunteers
joined other community members in the running of the
store—sorting donations and assisting customers. Once a
month, when the store was closed, CARDV clients could
go in and shop in privacy for free. Proceeds from the resale
shop benefited CARDV, Children's Farm Home, CASA,
and Jackson Street Youth Shelter.

Community Education

Half of CARDV's mission statement is "to provide education and leadership within the community to change the societal conditions that cultivate these forms of violence [sexual and domestic violence]." From the very earliest days, both of CARDV's mother agencies were presenting trainings to community members about the dynamics of sexual and domestic violence. In 1978 Corvallis Women Against Rape performed thirty speaking engagements with over 1,000 people in attendance—impressive statistics that could challenge what we are currently doing. During fiscal year 2014–2015, CARDV staff completed forty-two presentations and reached 1,168 individuals.

CURRENT TRAININGS

Advocacy Training
1977–Current

From the beginning the Rape Crisis Center and the Linn-Benton Association for the Prevention of Domestic Violence provided training to advocates.

When the Department of Human Services began allocating the Marriage License Tax funds and contracting with domestic violence and sexual assault programs in 1982, training requirements became standardized.

Today, all programs in the State of Oregon receiving Oregon Domestic and Sexual Violence Services Fund, Violence Against Women Act, Victims of Crime Act, and Department of Human Services funds are required to adhere to the DHS Advisory Committee's training guidelines. The standardized requirements insure that programs are utilizing best practices and the most current research available, and that programs throughout the state have a uniform base of proficiency and skill in responding to domestic violence, sexual assault and stalking. Advocates must complete the 40-hour training as well as numerous buddy shifts before working with survivors.

CARDV advocates never stop being trained. Inservices are held at weekly team meetings; whenever possible advocates attend state-wide trainings and conferences; and advocates routinely participate in webinars (trainings offered over Internet).

Community Trainings
1978–Current

CARDV trainings range from fifteen minute talks about CARDV services and how to access them, to hours-long presentations focusing on domestic violence, sexual assault, stalking, or sex trafficking. We can tailor each talk to the audience's needs and respond to requests from community and parent groups, educators, and students. We are also available to provide professional development for other agencies. All of CARDV's presentations are research-based.

In Her Shoes
2000–Current

Developed by the Washington Coalition Against Domestic Violence, In Her Shoes allows participants to "walk in the shoes" of a survivor of domestic violence.

Short narratives describing a survivor's experience, based on real-life events, are given to participants who are then challenged to make choices which will dictate their next steps. During the two-hour interactive exercise, participants gain powerful insight into the many barriers domestic violence survivors face every day.

In Her Shoes is used in CARDV's Advocacy Training for new staff and volunteers and is available for presentations to schools and the community.

In Their Shoes
2012–Current

In Their Shoes, developed by the Washington Coalition Against Domestic Violence, is an interactive exercise allowing participants to assume the roles of real teens experiencing dating violence, sexting, stalking, pregnancy, and homophobia.

Participants make choices about their relationship which move them through the scenario and its final outcome. The simulation gives participants a unique glimpse into what youth may face in their social world and the impact of violence.

In Their Shoes is available for presentations to schools and the community.

Past Trainings

International Training—Macedonia
March 2001

A joint project between CARDV and Oregon State University's Women in International Development brought eleven representatives from Macedonia to Corvallis for a three-week training. The Macedonians' goal was to change Macedonia's civil and criminal procedures to recognize and prosecute perpetrators of domestic violence.

Participants included a criminal judge, a deputy higher public prosecutor, a teacher, an attorney, the chief inspector in the Department for Juvenile Delinquency, the assistant minister at the Ministry of Justice, the president of a women's non-profit starting a hotline for female survivors of violence, and social workers from the Association for Emancipation, Solidarity and Equality of Women. Two interpreters traded off simultaneous interpreting duties.

The Macedonians were trained on domestic violence, sexual assault and stalking; toured CARDV's shelters; received information on hotline operation, legal advocacy, and hospital response; observed CARDV presentations at elementary and high schools; discussed fund-raising, volunteer coordination, and tools to raise public awareness. In addition, the group attended restraining order hearings and met with district attorneys, judges, law enforcement, and legislators.

Plain Talk
2002–2010

Plain Talk, Inc. began in 1994 as a pilot program of the Benton County Committee for the Prevention of Child Abuse. As community services expanded, Plain Talk incorporated, becoming one of only two agencies in the State to engage the whole community in child abuse prevention and intervention.

After suspending programs while seeking stable funding, Plain Talk determined that a new home with CARDV would allow the program to continue providing educational services to the community. In July of 2002 CARDV officially incorporated Plain Talk into CARDV's Community Education Program.

Designed for students in kindergarten through sixth grade, Plain Talk involved school personnel, parents, and the children themselves in lessening the child's vulnerability to violence. Classroom interactive presentations focused on the child's right to be safe, to be confident, and to make choices. Workshops for parents and school personnel were also offered.

By 2010 new research indicated the program was relying on outdated data and the decision was made to discontinue the program. CARDV provides schools with speakers and materials upon request.

Taking Action Against Dating Violence
2004–2010

Taking Action Against Dating Violence was a three-day program offered to middle and high school students. The first day examined gender stereotypes and how adherence to rigid gender roles can lead to inequality in relationships. Students also identified characteristics of unhealthy relationships. The second day provided comprehensive information on sexual assault. Day three addressed warning signs of an unhealthy relationship and bystander intervention strategies. The program concluded by generating characteristics of healthy relationships and ideas on how to support a survivor of sexual assault or dating violence.

While the program was successful in schools that permitted the entire program to be presented, most teachers preferred a one-hour talk instead. CARDV rewrote the curriculum into a shorter research-based presentation that can be more easily adapted to the timeframe requested.

Facilities

Blake House—Administrative Offices

On August 17, 1981, the Corvallis City Council unanimously approved the Housing and Community Development Committee recommendation to grant up to $100,000 to CARDV for the acquisition of a house to be used as confidential safe shelter.

After months of searching, we purchased a red brick house located at what was then the edge of town. The property had recently been annexed by the City of Corvallis and was the perfect location for a confidential shelter. Situated on Highway 20 on the way to the coast, houses were too far apart to define a neighborhood, and traffic moved fast enough that drivers didn't give much notice to anything they were speeding past. The administrative office remained in downtown Corvallis.

In the mid-1990s, the shelter was named for Faye

Blake, who had worked for the City of Corvallis and was instrumental securing the grant for CARDV. Ms. Blake also served on CARDV's board from 1982 through 1985, and guided us through those early, often tumultuous, years as we combined the ideologies of our two mother agencies and forged our new identity.

Built in 1948, the house had been a showplace in its day. A red brick wall framed and elevated the property from the surrounding fields. In the backyard, two cedar trees flanked bricked steps leading down to a barn and wheat field. The two-car garage was remodeled into a space for advocates to meet with shelter residents and answer the hotline. The family room, located in the full basement, became a children's area, with the wet bar a craft space. The attic stored bedding, toiletries, and a host of other supplies needed for the thousands of women and children who would eventually be residents.

We hauled an odd assortment of donated furniture into the house in January, 1982 to prepare for those first residents. There were so many donations we needed storage units for the overflow and were able to provide women leaving shelter with furniture and household necessities for months to come.

Two of the three bedrooms were set up with two bunk beds, with a trundle and single bed in the third bedroom for a total of eleven beds, plus cribs. Mismatched couches and overstuffed chairs filled the living room, and the table in the dining room was big enough for residents to share their eating space with whatever jigsaw puzzle was currently in progress.

In 1989 US West Telephone Company erroneously published the shelter's confidential address next to the crisis line number in the phone book. Advocates immediately painted a different house number on the dummy mailbox in front of the house. Motion sensor lights equipped with interior warning buzzers were installed around the property, and numerous, often heated, conversations ensued with US West about relocating the shelter. After lengthy negotiations, US West financed a state-of-the art alarm system and gave CARDV a one-year telephone credit.

For fourteen years the Blake House served as CARDV's only shelter. Then in 1996 an Oregon Housing and Community Services grant made it possible for us to obtain a second confidential shelter, the Pack House, and to remodel the Blake House and bring it up to current housing codes.

In November 1999, we were literally rained out of our downtown administrative office, which was located across the street from the Benton County Courthouse. The landlord had mounted new skylights in the roof, but had not yet installed the sealer before the heavy rains started. After four days of downpour, water seeped through the upstairs floor causing the water-logged ceiling tiles to fall in the downstairs CARDV offices. With the help of volunteers, staff evacuated the building—moving filing cabinets and furniture into storage, and setting up temporary offices in the Pack House, which fortunately housed no residents at the time. All meetings were held off site to protect the confidentiality of the location, and a vigorous hunt began for suitable office space.

After months of an unsuccessful search, the Board began questioning how confidential the Blake House still was after eighteen years. The decision was made to rent a house for use as a confidential shelter and convert the Blake House into CARDV's administrative offices. We rented a suitable house from a landlord who understood how crucial confidentiality was, and modifications began on the Blake House. An open house on June 22, 2000 officially announced the new role the Blake House would serve for CARDV.

Today, Fiscal Management, Development, and Shelter Services are housed at Blake, and the house is open to the public.

CONFIDENTIAL SHELTERS

Both of our shelters are residential homes blending into quiet Corvallis neighborhoods, within walking distance of bus stops and grocery stores. The two handicapped accessible shelters have a combined total of sixteen beds, not including cribs and emergency cots.

Pack House

The Pack House was donated to CARDV in 1996 and opened for residents in 1997. The house is named for Gay-Lynn Pack, CARDV's Executive Director from 1992 to 1998.

O'Mara House

A City of Corvallis Community Development Block Grant made it possible for CARDV to purchase the O'Mara

House and move out of the house we had been renting. After extensive remodeling, it was opened to residents in 2005. The house is named for Nancy O'Mara, CARDV's Executive Director from 2001 to 2010.

Advocacy Center

Opened in May 2012, the Advocacy Center was built in partnership with Willamette Neighborhood Housing as part of Alexander Court, an affordable housing development. Ten of the twenty-four units are reserved for survivors of domestic violence, with CARDV providing supportive services. The property for the Advocacy Center was purchased through a City of Corvallis Community Development Block Grant, and the building was made possible through the generous donations from community members and private foundations.

Located across the street from Lincoln School at 2208 SW Third Street, the Advocacy Center serves as the public face of CARDV. Meeting space is available for community partners, Legal Aid Services schedules regular appointment hours, and various classes and groups are offered for survivors of domestic and sexual violence.

The Advocacy Center houses our outreach services and provides on-going supportive services to survivors and their families. The visible and very public location has made us more accessible to the community than ever before.

Linn County Offices

CARDV's first Linn County office was opened in November 1992 in Lebanon. Open half time, the space was shared with Lebanon Basic Services, an information and referral agency. The following September the office was forced to close due to lack of funding.

CARDV's two AmeriCorps members opened an Albany office during the summer of 2000 in donated space at the newly-built Songbird Village, an affordable apartment complex. In October the following year, 2001, the office was moved to Two Rivers Market in Albany, where the Department of Human Services Self Sufficiency unit was temporarily housed. Since that time, we have staffed cubicles at Albany and Lebanon DHS offices from one to five days a week, depending upon available funding.

Currently, a contract with DHS provides for a full time advocate to split her time between the Albany and Lebanon DHS offices, and the Linn County Commissioners make space available at the courthouse for CARDV to meet with survivors whenever needed. Having advocates available in Linn County gives survivors more immediate access to our services. It is one of CARDV's short-term goals to have a "store-front" presence in Linn County.

Community Partnerships and Coalitions

Partnering with other agencies and coalitions has allowed CARDV to expand resources and services available to survivors. We connect with other agencies and businesses in Benton and Linn counties on a daily basis on behalf of our clients—including Community Outreach, Inc., Heartland Humane Society, Department of Human Services, the district attorneys' offices, law enforcement, area hospitals, and religious institutions, just to name a few.

Quilts From Caring Hands and the Zion Lutheran Church Quilters make sure that every adult and child in shelter is given their own quilt to keep. Shelter residents shop for free clothing and acquire household supplies for their new homes at Vina Moses; Love INC supplies survivors with bicycles and other needs; local hair dressers donate coupons for free hair cuts. This community support is vital for survivors who are rebuilding their lives.

PARTNERSHIPS AND COALITIONS

Oregon Coalition Against Domestic and Sexual Violence
1980–Current

CARDV has been a member of the Oregon Coalition Against Domestic and Sexual Violence since its incorporation in 1980.

Before 1980, domestic violence and sexual assault programs, scattered across the state, were often unaware of one another. The Coalition made an information sharing network possible and provided the technical support the fledgling programs needed.

In collaboration with other partners, the Coalition has been instrumental in the passage of major Oregon legislation: including emergency restraining orders for domestic violence, removal of the requirement to prove a rape was 'forcible,' and the Marriage License Tax to help fund domestic violence programs throughout the state.

Over the years, many CARDV staff members have attended and presented workshops at the Coalition's annual conference as well as served on the board of directors.

Department of Human Services (DHS)
Self Sufficiency and Child Welfare
2001–Current

CARDV staffed a cubicle two days a week at the Albany Department of Human Services beginning in October, 2001 when our outreach office moved from Songbird Village to DHS Self Sufficiency (which at that time was housed at Two Rivers Market). The following year, 2002, we began staffing a cubicle in Lebanon's DHS office one day a week. But it wasn't until 2004, when CARDV received a grant from DHS, that we were compensated for these services. For the next few years, depending upon DHS funding and available staffing, CARDV provided advocates from one to five days a week in Albany and Lebanon.

In 2011, CARDV received a two-year Intimate Partner Violence grant to work with pregnant and parenting teens. The grant, in partnership with DHS Self Sufficiency, Child Welfare, and Linn County Public Health, provided for a CARDV advocate to be stationed at the Albany DHS Office four days a week.

A 2014 three-year contract with DHS provided for a full time advocate to split her time between the Albany and Lebanon offices, and a half-time advocate in Corvallis.

Having an advocate on site at DHS means DHS and Child Welfare caseworkers can make immediate referrals. Advocates provide clients with crisis intervention, safety planning, resources and information, peer counseling, support during court hearings, and help with completing forms in order to access other services.

Willamette Neighborhood Housing
2002–Intermittent

In 2002, CARDV met with Willamette Neighborhood Housing to explore the feasibility of building transitional housing for survivors of domestic violence. Thus began many discussions about supportive housing services (as it is now called), inspections of properties and buildings for sale, and searches for possible funding—finally culminating in the CARDV Advocacy Center and Alexander Court opening in 2012. Ten of the twenty-four units in Alexander Court are set aside for survivors of domestic violence, with CARDV providing the supportive services.

The Advocacy Center and Alexander Court wasn't the first time Willamette Neighborhood Housing stepped up to support us. When CARDV was looking to purchase our second shelter in 2003, their technical assistance was invaluable—inspecting properties with us and even going so far as gaining their board approval for purchasing a house on our behalf if by chance we were to find the perfect location before our funding was secured.

Sexual Assault Response Teams (SARTS)
2003–Current (Benton County)
2004–Current (Linn County)

The first Sexual Assault Response Team (SART) began in 1975 in Memphis, Tennessee. The Memphis Police Department recognized that a collaborative response to sexual assault and increased training would result in better victim support, better investigations, and better prosecutions. The first Sexual Assault Nurse Examiner program was developed as part of the SART effort.

The SART concept was slow to move across the country. In 1999 Oregon Attorney General Hardy Myers convened the first statewide Sexual Assault Summit. This led to the formation of the Sexual Assault Task Force, established to look at the problem of low reporting of sexual assaults and to provide state-wide trainings for law enforcement, district attorneys, victims assistance and sexual assault programs. In the early 2000s, Hardy Myers made the creation of SARTs a priority for every county in the state.

In 2004 Hardy Myers established the Oregon Sexual Assault Examiner/Sexual Assault Nurse Examiner Certification Commission. Oregon is one of only seven states that offer state-level certification. Letetia Wilson, CARDV's Executive Director, serves on the Commission.

Sexual Assault Response Teams work hard to ensure that sexual assault survivors receive the respect, support and access to services they deserve. The victim-centered approach gives survivors back a measure of the control that was taken away during the assault, and allows them to make better informed choices about reporting.

Coalition Against Human Trafficking
2011–Current

The Coalition Against Human Trafficking was organized in 2011 with the mission to positively impact Linn and Benton counties' response to young victims of human trafficking through education, training and resources. In 2013 the Coalition requested CARDV to assume the leadership of the group. CARDV was already a participating member of the Coalition and since we were responding to a majority of the requests for speakers and information, it was a natural fit. CARDV has worked with survivors of sex trafficking since 1981.

Men Ending Violence Coalition
2012–Current

The Men Ending Violence Coalition is a CARDV-sponsored men's resource group dedicated to shifting the cultural norms that support violence against women and girls. Coalition members facilitate dialogue with community groups, schools, faith-based groups, and other organizations to explore male identity and men's violence and offer workshops on healthy masculinity and violence prevention.

Working with Teens
2013–Current

CARDV partners with other agencies who are working with teen girls who are at risk and therefore especially vulnerable and likely to be survivors. In 2013, we started Girls Circle in conjunction with ABC House (All Because of Children), the child abuse intervention center serving Linn and Benton counties. CARDV also facilitates groups for teen girls at YES House for Teens (Youth Entering Sobriety), and meets one-on-one with youth at the Oak Creek Youth Correctional Facility.

Legal Assistance for Victims
2015–Current

A grant through the Office on Violence Against Women made it possible for Legal Aid Services of Oregon to partner with CARDV and the Center for Hope and Safety in Salem to provide civil legal services to victims of domestic violence and sexual assault in the mid-Willamette Valley region of Oregon. The program focus is elders, people with disabilities, Latinos, and victims in rural areas. Each partner's existing services were expanded to include effective protocol to identify potential legal issues that victims may need to resolve in order to achieve safety and stability.

PAST PARTNERSHIPS AND COALITIONS

Women In Transition FIRE Project
1992–1997

Community Outreach, Inc. and CARDV pooled resources to establish the Women In Transition FIRE Project: FIRE standing for Freedom, Independence, Renewal, and Empowerment. Shelter residents interested in the program met with Community Outreach's case manager and CARDV's counselor for on-going transitional services including: counseling, case management, children's counseling, child care, transportation, housing search assistance, education, job training referrals, and support groups. Clients were able to participate in as many of the services offered by FIRE as they wished, and for as long as they found the program helpful.

Partnership for Safe Families
August 1995–February 1996

As part of a State-wide effort to improve services to women and children living in domestic violence, CARDV, in collaboration with the Benton County Branch of Children's Services Division (now Department of Human Services Child Welfare Office), was chosen to participate in a six-month pilot project by the Department of Human Services. The National Center for Child Abuse and Neglect funded the project and the Oregon Coalition Against Domestic and Sexual Violence administered the funds.

A CARDV advocate was stationed at Children's Services and accompanied the caseworker to the home in cases of domestic violence. The project provided domestic violence training for Children's Services caseworkers and law enforcement, age appropriate treatment groups for child survivors of domestic violence, and safety planning, advocacy, and support for the mothers.

A training video outlining how this pilot project worked was provided to every Children's Services Division office and domestic violence program in Oregon.

Family Violence Councils
1996–early 2000s

Both Linn and Benton counties established Family Violence Councils to implement a coordinated community response in identifying and closing the gaps in survivor and offender services. A Byrne Grant provided for a CARDV-based coordinator for the Benton County Family Violence

Council, and Linn County Victims Assistance coordinated the Linn County Council. Among the many members were district attorneys, Victims Assistance, law enforcement, batterer intervention programs, judges, Legal Aid, Senior Services, Department of Human Services, CARDV, ABC House, Community Outreach, Inc., as well as schools and community members.

The councils made recommendations to the judiciary on batterer treatment programs, and conducted a mandatory reporter survey on child abuse. Most importantly, the councils brought people together to discuss family violence. The "Check Up on Your Relationship" cards designed by the Councils are still among CARDV's most frequently requested printed materials.

When the Byrne grant was not renewed, the Willamette Criminal Justice Council picked up the Benton County Council.

Senior Safe Passages
1998–2000

CARDV collaborated with Cascades West Senior Services in the creation of Senior Safe Passages, a two and-a-half year project funded by a Victims of Crime Act Demonstration Grant from the Oregon Department of Justice.

Senior Safe Passages addressed the needs of women aged 60 or older who were living in domestic violence. The grant funded a full-time older battered women's service coordinator stationed at Cascades West Senior Services, who could respond in the home to women needing crisis intervention services. The service coordinator attended

CARDV's weekly advocacy meetings and CARDV participated on the Elder Multi-Disciplinary Team. CARDV and Senior Services presented trainings throughout the state on services for older battered women.

To accommodate the needs of older survivors of domestic violence, we opened our shelter doors to allow for in-home health care service providers and created the option of a child-free quiet space.

Community Awareness

Demonstrations, Candlelight Vigils, Speak Outs
1977–Intermittent

Demonstrations, candlelight vigils, and speak outs are the mainstays of any grassroots movement. In the 1970s and 80s and even into the early 90s, we stood on the street in front of the Linn and Benton County courthouses with signs proclaiming "Violence Against Women is Wrong—Stop it!" and handed out leaflets. For many community members, this was the first time they had heard such radical statements. Now, our newly formed Coalition Against Human Trafficking is following suit with their own demonstrations.

More situation-focused demonstrations and vigils have ranged from protesting *Playboy Magazine* when they came to photograph Oregon State University women students in 1993 to the 1996 event in front of the Benton County courthouse after the announcement of the O. J. Simpson verdict. Over two hundred people attended that rally and more people signed up for our volunteer training than at any other time in our history.

Demonstrations are designed to not only raise awareness in the community, but also to give participants an opportunity to express their own hopes, frustrations and passions around the issues of sexual and domestic violence.

Today, in keeping with the times, most demonstrations have moved from the streets to online.

Linn County Events
1979–Current

With CARDV's permanent offices and shelters all located in Corvallis, we make an extra effort to remind people that we serve Linn County too. In addition to staffing cubicle space at the Department of Human Services in Linn County and being in the courthouse every morning to assist with protection orders, we've hosted dinners and awareness events in Albany, Lebanon and Sweet Home. Local businesses assist us by displaying our literature and donating a portion of their day's business proceeds to us.

More than 50 percent of our clients and crisis line calls come from Linn County.

Awareness Months
National Events
1981–Current

By 1984, the National Coalition Against Domestic Violence had expanded what had begun as "Day of Unity" in October 1981 into National Domestic Violence Week. It was first observed as Domestic Violence Awareness Month in October, 1987. Multiple other awareness months highlighting domestic and sexual violence followed.

In 1984, during the first national Domestic Violence Awareness Week, NBC aired *The Burning Bed*, the story of Francine Hughes, a battered woman from Lancing, Michigan who was tried for first degree murder in 1977. The movie was ground-breaking in that a graphic depiction of the reality of domestic violence had never before been seen on television. Ms. Hughes, after being battered by her husband for thirteen years, and after repeated failed attempts to escape his violence, finally resorted to setting his bed on fire while he slept. She was found not guilty by reason of temporary insanity. The case set a legal precedent.

At the end of *The Burning Bed*, local stations showed CARDV's phone number along with Mid-Valley Women's Crisis Service in Salem (now Center for Hope and Safety) and WomenSpace in Eugene. The following year, during Domestic Violence Week, Oregon Governor Victor Atiyeh declared October 12, 1985 as "Unity for Battered Women and Victims of Sexual Assault Day."

During Awareness Months, CARDV has held speak outs, participated in panel discussions, hosted films, created window displays in local businesses, and distributed informational bookmarks at libraries and bookstores.

Awareness Months for issues relating to domestic and sexual violence include:

Domestic Violence Awareness—October, purple ribbon. First observed in 1981.

Child Abuse Awareness—April, blue ribbon. First observed in 1983.

Sexual Assault Awareness—April, teal ribbon. First observed in 2001.

Stalking Awareness—January, silver ribbon. First observed in 2004.

Teen Dating Violence Awareness—February, orange ribbon. First observed in 2006.

Sex Trafficking Awareness—January, blue ribbon. First observed in 2007.

Bathroom Stickers
1984–Current

A creative way to reach potential survivors has been through CARDV's Bathroom Sticker Campaign. In the early days, if we had asked local businesses for permission to install the stickers, we would have most likely been refused. So the stickers were primarily installed by stealth. Not all businesses were forgiving, as in the case of US West Telephone Company, who in 1985 informed us that if we didn't stop putting our stickers in their phone booths they would start charging us to remove them.

Today, we often receive requests from area businesses for the stickers. It's a great project for community groups or students seeking a political action activity. Many of our clients have said they first learned of our hotline through a bathroom sticker.

Take Back the Night March
National Event
1985–Current

The first Take Back the Night March in the United States was held in 1978 in San Francisco's pornography district to protest the pornography industry and the role it plays in violence against women. More than 5,000 women from thirty states attended. The event now takes place all over the country.

The march is a time to protest violence against women and the beliefs, attitudes and behaviors that perpetuate sexual violence. It takes place at night to symbolize women's reclaiming their personal power during the timeframe most women have been taught to fear. It is a powerful way for survivors and supporters to break the silence around violence against women. Male allies support the participants by choosing to either march behind the women, or not to march at all—recognizing that the event is about women taking action for themselves.

Marchers, carrying candles or flashlights, wind their way through the dark city streets shouting, "Yes means yes, no means no / However we dress, wherever we go!" and other chants. At the march's conclusion, survivors and supporters can participate in a speak out, sharing personal experiences or short speeches about violence against women.

CARDV participates by serving on Take Back the Night March planning committees, attending the march, sometimes serving as keynote speaker, and often speaking during the speak out. The event is typically held in Corvallis during April, Sexual Assault Awareness Month.

Silent Witness Exhibit
National Event
1997–Intermittent

In August of 1990 over lunch, a small group of women artists and writers at an art college in Minneapolis discussed the number of murders that had occurred over the summer as a result of domestic violence. Out of this discussion came the Silent Witness exhibit. The following February, more than 500 women met at the Minnesota State Capital and marched with twenty-seven Silent Witness figures, single file, through the State Capital to protest violence against women.

Silent Witnesses are life-sized blood-red painted silhouettes of women who were killed by domestic violence. Each witness bears a gold shield over her heart inscribed with her name and the circumstances of her death.

By 1997 all fifty states had created Silent Witness exhibits honoring the women who died from their own state. WomenSpace, the domestic violence program in Eugene, and the Oregon Coalition Against Domestic and Sexual Violence made Oregon the seventh state to establish an exhibit. On October 18, 1997, 1,500 Silent Witnesses from all fifty states joined the March to End the Silence in Washington DC to raise awareness about domestic violence.

Silent Witnesses have accompanied CARDV to speak outs, Take Back the Night Marches, and other demonstrations.

During the year 2013, domestic violence-related deaths claimed 36 in Oregon.

Denim Day
National Event
1999–Current

In 1997, an 18-year-old girl was raped and abandoned by a 45-year-old perpetrator in an alley in Rome, Italy. He was convicted of rape and sentenced to jail. Months later, he appealed and the case made it all the way to the Italian Supreme Court. Within a matter of days the case was overturned, dismissed, and the perpetrator released. The Head Judge argued, "Because the victim wore very, very tight jeans, she had to help him remove them … and by removing the jeans … it was no longer rape but consensual sex." Within hours the women in the Italian Parliament protested by wearing jeans to work. The California Senate and Assembly was inspired to follow suit in 1999 and Denim Day was born.

Typically held on a Friday in April, Sexual Assault Awareness Month, CARDV participates by encouraging our friends, family, supporters and community partners to wear denim that day.

Clothesline Project
International Event
1999–Intermittent

The Clothesline Project is a moving exhibition of shirts — each created by, or on behalf of, a woman who has been the victim of sexual or domestic violence, stalking, or sex trafficking. Shirts are pinned shoulder to shoulder on clotheslines and shown at demonstrations around the country. Originated by the Cape Cod Women's Agenda in 1990, the Clothesline is a powerful visual testament to the prevalence of violence against women. Portland area women began a Clothesline Project in 1991, and other cities around the state created their own Clotheslines soon after.

Shirts are embellished with messages, poems, pictures or whatever is meaningful to the survivor. Color-fast dyes, fabric pens, paints, and collage are used. No shirt is ever rejected on the basis of design.

During October's Domestic Violence Awareness Month in 1999, CARDV hosted an evening for survivors in the community to make T-shirts for the Project, and Oregon State University Women's Center has sponsored a number of events.

Throughout the 1990s and early 2000s, a Clothesline was frequently exhibited at the State Capital when bills concerning violence against women were being considered at the Legislature.

Door-to-Door Campaign to End Violence
2000–2001

More than 200 volunteers distributed door hangers in Corvallis neighborhoods on a Saturday morning during Domestic Violence Awareness Month in 2000. The awareness event was repeated the following year in Corvallis and also in Albany. The door hangers featured information on domestic violence and a tear-off postcard listing suggestions on how the recipient could support survivors.

The Vagina Monologues
International Event
2001–Intermittent

Eve Ensler began writing *The Vagina Monologues* in 1996 after interviewing more than 200 women about sex, relationships, and violence. Consisting of a series of monologues delivered by an individual or several women facing the audience, the Vagina Monologues has become its own movement to stop violence against women.

The play is typically staged during February, often on Valentine's Day, with proceeds going to support local sexual assault and domestic violence agencies around the world. Oregon State University produced the play for a number of years with CARDV as the primary beneficiary; and local thespians have staged performances at the Majestic Theater in Corvallis.

Poster Contest—Sexual Assault Awareness Month
2006–2010

The Poster Contest was open to all high school students in Linn and Benton counties. Reproductions of the winning posters were distributed for display in local high schools to raise awareness about the dynamics and prevalence of sexual assault in our community as well as to provide students with CARDV's 24-hour hotline number. The winning poster was featured on our website and in our newsletter.

Online Presence
2007–Current

Until a couple of volunteers who designed websites for a living offered to create a site for CARDV, the closest we came to having a media presence were a few public service announcements that ran on local cable access channels in 2002.

Our website went live in 2007 and by 2009 CARDV was blogging, Facebooking, and tweeting. CARDV's website can reach more people with more information than our newsletter (which is still available by mail) ever could. In addition to announcements about upcoming events, viewers can learn about our services and the dynamics of sexual and domestic violence, and access resources. The video shown at our annual Breakfast for Safe Families can be seen as well.

Over a thousand people follow CARDV on Facebook

and each month close to two thousand people access our webpage.

Parades
2011–2014

In 1985, CARDV's executive director stuck a CARDV sign on her pickup truck and drove it in the Benton County United Way Parade. A few volunteers accompanied her and handed out CARDV literature.

Twenty-six years later, in 2011, the Linn County Outreach Committee decided that participating in parades would be a good way for CARDV to gain visibility in Linn County. The tropical paradise-themed float for the Lebanon Strawberry Festival was the first effort. Everyone wore their "I ♥ CARDV" T-shirts and marched down Highway 20 with the float. The "Everyone Deserves to be Safe" float in the Albany Veterans Day Parade followed in November, along with a third place trophy. Heady with success, the Linn County volunteers built award-winning floats for the Sweet Home Sportsman Parade, as well as subsequent Strawberry Festivals, Veterans Day, and Lebanon Twilight parades. Marchers passed out paper flags with CARDV's phone number to attendees along the way.

The events were about a lot more than just building clever floats, winning trophies and smiling and waving to the folks lining the streets. After one event, a woman called our hotline saying she heard about us from a flag she had gotten at the parade. And who knows how many others learned about us the same way.

One-in-Four Display
2015–Current

The One-in-Four Display consists of four life-sized sil-houettes, three painted purple and one white. "1 in 4" is marked boldly across the chest of the white silhouette, with the accompanying placard announcing, "1 in 4 women will experience domestic violence in their lifetime." The display is a powerful and sobering visual representation.

The display was introduced in Linn County in 2015 during October, Domestic Violence Awareness Month, and travelled to various locations, including the Lebanon Public Library, the Heritage Mall, and the community-wide candlelight vigil honoring survivors at the Linn County Courthouse.

Plans are underway to create a similar display for Benton County.

Legislation

L egislation is crucial to legitimize a social change movement. To quote Supreme Court Justice Sonia Sotomayer,
"Through law, you could change the very structure of
society and the way communities functioned."

In addition to letter-writing and e-mail campaigns,
CARDV attends the Domestic Violence, Sexual Assault
and Stalking Awareness Days at the State Capitol each
legislative session. This is an excellent opportunity to meet
with our legislators and urge them to support survivors by
increasing funding to sexual and domestic violence programs and passing legislation that will provide survivors
with greater protections.

CARDV also participates in surveys that the Oregon
Alliance to End Violence Against Women initiates to
identify the priority issues facing survivors. The Alliance,
founded in 1999, is a grassroots organization dedicated to

promoting legislation in Oregon that protects and empowers survivors. CARDV advocates work with the Alliance by providing testimony to the Legislature in support of particular bills.

SELECTED NOTEWORTHY OREGON LEGISLATION

1977—Oregon adopts the Family Abuse Protection Act (FAPA).

1978—Oregon becomes the first state to make marital rape a crime. Benton County District Attorney Pete Sandrock is instrumental in the law's passage.

1979—HB 2104: Allows a person who formerly cohabited with another to obtain a temporary restraining order or other remedies available under the Family Abuse Prevention Act.

1981—SB 355, 356, and 358: Amendments to the Family Abuse Prevention Act: Expands the act to include not only spouse, former spouses, or cohabitants, but also the elderly, adult children, and marital rape victims. Creates a uniform statewide response procedure to family violence and enables victims to obtain a restraining order without the assistance of an attorney.

1989—SB 479: Allows a person seeking a restraining order to have the court order police to accompany them to the residence to retrieve personal belongings.

1991—HB 2407: Requires lifetime registration of sex offenders. Parole officers are responsible for entering data on sex offenders into law enforcement data system computer, including the offender's name and description, a description of the methodology of the crime, their address and any address changes.

1999—Rev. Stat. 163.160(3)(c): Makes domestic violence a felony charge if a child living in the household witnesses the abuse.

1999—SB 944: Makes changes to sexual offense statute and to Oregon's evidence code. Omits the requirement that a rape victim "earnestly resist" her attacker.

1999—SB 1202: Creates a Sexual Assault Victim's fund from Oregon's percentage of the Criminal Fines and Assessment Account.

1999—HB-2464: Adds persons with disabilities to the Elder Abuse Restraining Order, now called Elderly Persons and Persons with Disabilities Abuse Prevention Act.

2001—HB 2767: Allows victims to stay away from work and collect unemployment benefits if they are not able to work due to the threat of violence by a domestic partner.

2003—HB 2770: Creates a new crime of strangulation.

2005—HB 2662: Expands and solidifies the protections in unemployment benefits law to allow victims of domestic violence, sexual assault, or stalking to qualify for benefits if they must quit work for safety reasons.

2005—HB 3486: Requires Oregon State Police to post information on the Internet pertaining to predatory or sexual violent sex offenders.

2005—SB 106: Expands the definition of abuse in the Elderly Persons and Persons with Disabilities Abuse Prevention Act to include non-consenting sexual contact.

2005—SB 198: Allows victims of certain person crimes to select a "personal representative" to accompany them to all phases of the investigation, medical examination, and prosecution related to the criminal incident.

2005—SB 243: Prohibits persons convicted of certain sex crimes from being present at or on property adjacent to the grounds of a school, child care center, playground or other places intended for use primarily by children, without prior written approval.

2005—SB 850: Creates the Address Confidentiality Program in the Department of Justice for victims of domestic violence, sexual assault, and stalking. Provides victims with a P.O. box at the Attorney General's office which they may use as their official address.

2005—SB 983: Protects access to local residential and toll-free telephone services for victims who are at risk of violence.

2005—SB 1047: Creates the authority and protocols for local communities to convene multi-disciplinary review of records related to domestic violence fatalities for the purpose of preventing future deaths.

2007—HB 2153: Eliminates the criminal statute of limitations for certain sex crimes in cases in which the perpetrator's DNA has been collected.

2007—HB 2154: Eliminates the requirement for law enforcement authorization prior to collection of an Oregon State Police Sexual Assault Forensic Exam, so that victims of sexual assault can obtain a forensic exam regardless of whether they have decided to report the crime to law enforcement.

2007—HB 2700: Requires hospitals to inform victims of sexual assault about emergency contraception and treatment options and to provide emergency contraception upon request by victims.

2007—HB 2869: Authorizes law enforcement to forcibly enter specified premises to enforce an order of assistance pertaining to custody, or to enforce a Family Abuse Prevention Act custody provision.

2007—SB 578: Creates the crime of subjecting another person to involuntary servitude, and the crime of trafficking in persons.

2007—SB 946: Requires employers to provide unpaid leave for survivors of domestic violence, sexual assault or stalking for the purpose of seeking legal or law enforcement help, seeking medical attention, obtaining services from a crisis center, obtaining psychological counseling, or relocating or securing a current home.

2009—HB 2343: Changes definition of "mental incapacitation" for purposes of Oregon's sexual assault laws to include any incapacitation that results in the victim's inability to consent. The bill removes the question of how a person who is assaulted became incapacitated, and focuses instead on the person's ability to consent to sexual activity and the defendant's knowledge of that state of mental incapacity.

2009—HB 3273: Provides statutory authority for Department of Human Services to contract with non-profit victim services providers to place domestic violence advocates at child welfare offices to provide safety and support services to parents in the system who are victims of domestic violence.

2009—SB 839: Adds victims of human trafficking to those qualified for the Address Confidentiality Program.

2009—SB 928: Prohibits employers from refusing to hire an otherwise qualified individual because that person is a victim of domestic violence, sexual assault, or stalking; and may not discharge, demote, suspend, or in any manner discriminate or retaliate against an individual because that person is a victim.

2010—HB 3623: Requires Oregon Liquor Control Commission to include informational materials regarding human trafficking with certain license renewals, if the materials are provided by a non-profit advocacy organization.

2010—HB 3651: Expands insurance discrimination protections currently available to domestic violence victims to sexual assault victims.

2011—HB 2244: Exempts records of a domestic or sexual violence service or resource centers sponsored by public agencies from public records laws.

2011—HB 2714: Creates separate crime of "patronizing a prostitute" with heightened fine for patronizing a minor. Ignorance of age is not a defense.

2011—HB 2940: Increases the classification of the crime of strangulation from a Class A misdemeanor to a Class C felony in certain circumstances. Adds strangulation to the list of crimes requiring mandatory arrest if committed by a family member against a family member.

2011—SB 425: Expands the crime of compelling prostitution to include an instance when a person knowingly aids or facilitates the commission of prostitution by a person under 18 years of age. Ignorance of age is not a defense.

2011—SB 557: Directs the district attorney in each county to organize a Sexual Assault Response Team (SART). A SART Team consists of representatives from the district attorney's office, a prosecution-based victim assistance program, the county sheriff's office or local law enforcement or both, a nonprofit agency program that receives DHS victim service funds, and a sexual assault forensic examiner.

2011—SB 616: Adds a provision in the Family Abuse Prevention Act for the judge to grant "other relief that the court considers necessary to ... prevent the neglect and protect the safety of any service or therapy animal or any animal kept for personal protection or companionship."

2012—HB 4077: Directs each school district board to adopt policies and curricula regarding teen dating and sexual violence. Each policy must state that teen dating violence and sexual violence is prohibited and each student has a right to a safe learning environment.

2012—HB 4146: Allows a person who was charged with or convicted of the crime of prostitution, when the person was less than 18 years old at the time of the offense, to obtain an expunction of the record.

2013—HB 2226: Prohibits a court from requiring public notice and posting of a change of name application if the applicant is a certified adult participant in the Address Confidentiality Program, unless good cause exists to require notice.

2013—HB 2779: Establishes authority for a Sexual Abuse Protective Order to protect victims of sexual abuse who are not eligible for a Family Abuse Prevention Act restraining order.

2015—HB 2317: Extends the statute of limitations for certain sex crimes from six to twelve years after commission of the crime.

2015—HB 2356: Upgrades the crime of invasion of personal privacy. Creates higher sanctions when the invasion is caused by someone knowingly recording another in a state of nudity without consent and when there is a reasonable expectation of privacy.

2015—HB 2758: Provides for sexual assault exam information to go directly to the patient, rather than the insurance policy holder.

2015—HB 2776: Allows law enforcement to issue emergency restraining orders, effective for seven judicial business days, giving victims more time to get to the courthouse and apply for a Family Abuse Prevention Act restraining order.

2015—HB 3466: Provides that the release decision for a defendant charged with a sex crime or crime constituting domestic violence must include order prohibiting attempted contact with victim and third-party contact with victim while defendant is in custody.

2015—HB 3468: Amends the crime of coercion to include threatening to cause physical injury to an animal in order to induce another person to engage in conduct.

2015—HB 3469: Increases penalty for crime of strangulation when committed knowing victim was pregnant.

2015—HB 3476: Grants certified advocates privilege from disclosing communications from domestic violence, sexual assault or stalking survivors without their consent.

2015—SB 3: Creates the crime of endangering a person protected by a Family Abuse Prevention Act restraining order when the order is violated.

2015—SB 188: Creates crime of unlawful dissemination of intimate images.

2015—SB 199: Requires the State Board of Parole and Post-Prison Supervision to notify the victim, if requested, prior to hearing or administrative decision to reset or advance the release date of a prisoner for outstanding reformation, severe medical condition or age-related incapacity.

2015—SB 390: Prohibits landlords from billing a survivor for damage done by the perpetrator.

2015—SB 454: Requires all employers to implement sick time for employees. The bill specifies that Domestic Violence/Sexual Assault safe leave qualifies as sick leave.

2015—SB 492: Authorizes use of accrued sick leave or personal business leave by certain employees who are victims of domestic violence, harassment, sexual assault or stalking.

2015—SB 525B: Prohibits possession of firearm or ammunition by person who is subject to a restraining order issued by court under Family Abuse Prevention Act or who has been convicted of certain misdemeanor crimes involving domestic violence.

2015—SB 788: Requires petitioners in family law proceedings to disclose protective orders.

2015—SB 790: Requires school district boards to adopt policies that incorporate age-appropriate education about domestic violence into training programs for students in grades seven through twelve and school employees.

Part Three
The Future

Towards That
Glorious Day

The opening of the Advocacy Center in May of 2012 launched a new era for CARDV.

For the first time, "CARDV" is emblazoned across the front of our building in letters large enough for passing traffic to easily recognize. The Advocacy Center's very visible and public location, at a bus stop on SW Third Street in Corvallis, allows us to open our facilities to our community partners. Now the resources can come to our clients.

All over the country, domestic and sexual violence programs are placing advocates in newly established Family Justice Centers. These centers offer a multitude of services where survivors of sexual assault and domestic violence can file police reports, get protection orders, meet with human services, safety plan with advocates, and complete intakes for confidential shelter.

Rarely a day passes that incidences of domestic violence,

sexual assault, stalking, sex trafficking, or the sexual abuse of children are not in the news. While some still persist in judging the victim to be at fault, more and more people are likely to believe her and express outrage against perpetrators. Pop singers and movie stars speak out against sexism, domestic and sexual violence, and raise money to fight sex trafficking. President Obama launched the "It's On Us" campaign to end sexual assault on college campuses.

It would seem that the movement to end violence against women has gone mainstream.

Women have made enormous strides during the last thirty-five years. The number of women in professional fields has increased significantly and in 2014 women made up 20 percent of Congress, five times the number in 1978. Women serve in the military, are airline pilots, doctors and dentists, full time mothers, bankers, entrepreneurs.

And yet.

Over fifty years after the Equal Pay Act, women still earn less than their male counterparts. In Oregon in 2013, the median earnings of women working full time as compared with men's was 80 percent. In the teaching professions nationwide, women earn 80.9 percent of their male co-workers' incomes. And despite the fact that since 1980 more women than men enrolled in higher education and graduated with honors, the leading occupations for women have remained virtually unchanged since 1960: secretaries, nurses, elementary and middle school teachers, cashiers and retail clerks.

Advertising continues to portray women and girls as

being sexually available and not really meaning "no" when they say it. At its worst, ads depict women as being battered, about to be raped, or even dead. Many rock music videos (which were originated by the advertising industry), graphically interweave sexual images with violence. Pornography is one of the fastest growing industries in the world. Pimps and sex trafficking are romanticized: "It's Hard Out Here for a Pimp" won the Academy Award for Best Original Song in 2006, and *Pretty Woman* is still rated as one of the most popular films of all time.

Misogyny thrives. Congress and individual states are steadily eroding reproductive rights, and abortion is becoming increasingly criminalized. Cutbacks to welfare, whose recipients are primarily women, are being enacted across the country. Diehard critics persist in the belief that feminists are to blame for the violence against women. Even though it has been demonstrated that feminism has improved our quality of life, many still denounce it.

In spite of increased laws to protect survivors from domestic and sexual violence, far too many district attorneys across the country are still unwilling to stand by the survivor and hold the perpetrator accountable. This reinforces the perpetrator's belief that he has the right to inflict violence on his victim. The survivor learns that the system can't, or won't, help her and she will be less likely to reach out for assistance in the future.

At the beginning of each Advocacy Training we include a section on the history of CARDV. Most advocates new to our work don't remember a time before services existed for sexual assault and domestic violence survivors. And unless they have taken women's studies classes at a university, they are not aware that our work is a key component in the social change movement to end violence against women.

Having no awareness of, or ignoring, the existing social structure that fosters violence against women, and focusing solely on services, one runs the risk of approaching each survivor from a therapeutic standpoint. In worst cases, it can lead to blaming the victim.

CARDV's feminist roots and grassroots history is the foundation that our philosophy and decision-making and survivor services are built upon.

Without acknowledging and cherishing our roots, in time the social change aspect of our work would be lost. And without that, we would become just another social service agency—providing a valuable service, but contributing nothing towards changing the societal conditions that created the need for our work to begin with.

Make no mistake: CARDV, along with the thousands of other sexual and domestic violence agencies across the country, is changing the course of history.

Legislation has been passed establishing protections for victims of domestic violence, sexual assault, stalking, sex trafficking, and sexual harassment. Federal and State funding has been created to help support services for survivors. The public's understanding of domestic and sexual violence has increased—survivors' disclosures are no longer so easily dismissed. Universities have protocols and policies in place to respond to sexual assault or sexual misconduct and stalking, and many have a Sexual Assault Nurse Examiner in their student health centers. Medical professionals routinely screen for domestic violence.

We have helped create a climate where sexual and domestic violence are no longer secrets.

Survivors now have language to describe what they are experiencing—thirty-five years ago, they just had a vague sense that something in their relationship wasn't right. Parents have the tools to talk to their kids about inappropriate touch. Acquaintance rape and healthy relationships can be discussed in middle and high schools. Universities offer courses on violence against women.

And still, there is much left to do.

We are often asked if we have seen a decrease in sexual assault and domestic violence incidents over the years. The question is usually asked with a hint of hopefulness—that after years of community education, building partnerships with law enforcement and other community partners, advocating for legislation that would provide greater protections for survivors—surely there has been a significant reduction in the need for our services.

The good news is that according to the U.S. Department of Justice, domestic violence incidents committed by intimate partners declined 63 percent from 1994 to 2012. This is comparable to the decline in the overall violent crime rate—67 percent.

If you look at the statistics CARDV compiles each month, however, it would appear that domestic and sexual violence is steadily holding, or in some years, rising.

More than likely, it is the reports of violence that have increased, rather than the number of incidents. Thirty-five years ago domestic and sexual violence was shrouded in secrecy and shame and very few women in Linn and Benton counties even knew there were services available that could assist them. Today, even if the survivor is unaware of our services, chances are good that her neighbor or co-worker or doctor or mother or religious leader can guide her to CARDV.

CARDV's outreach, including: legal advocacy every day at both Linn and Benton County courthouses to assist with protection orders; outreach offices at the Department of Human Services in Lebanon, Albany, and Corvallis; on-scene response with law enforcement, area hospitals and other medical facilities; information booths at fairs, newspaper articles, brochures, and bathroom stickers—has introduced thousands of survivors to our services.

Efforts across the country, utilizing Jacquelyn C. Campbell's Danger Assessment Tool and the Lethality Assessment Program, both used by CARDV in partnership with law enforcement, have reduced the number of domestic violence homicides. Both tools have given law enforcement, as well as advocates, a consistent method to discuss risk factors facing survivors and to better safety plan.

When we look at our statistics each month and see an increase in the volume of our crisis and support line calls, number of shelter residents and bed nights, or any of our other services, we don't interpret it as a failing on our part or that of the movement. Instead, we are encouraged that more people are aware that help is available.

CARDV has always had strong male allies, but it wasn't until 2012—when the Men's Coalition to End Violence was established — that they came together in a focused effort to unite in our mission.

Violence against women is the end result of a social structure where one gender has power over the other. The underlying message in much of advertising, movies, television, sports, and computer gaming is that our culture places a high value on violence and the men who use it to maintain dominance.

If we are going to radically reduce the rates of violence against women, we need to confront the sexist norms men have been bombarded with since they were children. Most men are uncomfortable when they hear other men make derogatory remarks about women or witness their treatment of women. Often they think they are the only ones uneasy with the situation so they don't speak up. And, because this is the societal norm in which they live, most likely they wouldn't know what to say.

The Men's Coalition to End Violence is a CARDV-sponsored group whose goal is to educate and motivate men to join women in ending violence and discrimination against girls and women. The Men's Coalition works to increase awareness of gender-based violence, educate community members on the root causes of violence, and promote healthier definitions of masculinity.

Men are encouraged to "take a self-assessment of our fears about our own masculinity; make a commitment to talk with other men about masculinity and in particular, men's violence; spend some time thinking about the messages you've been given over your lifetime about masculinity and decide which are not useful to you or fair to women and children, then challenge those messages as you live your life."

Members of the Men's Coalition facilitate trainings in schools and the community to explore male identity and men's violence, and offer workshops on healthy masculinity and violence prevention.

This is the kind of work that has the potential for real change in our communities.

Over the years there has been a shift in CARDV's approach to social change work. Some would say we've become more "professional." Others would counter that we've lost our edge.

It's true that not all of the community partners who work with domestic and sexual violence survivors share CARDV's ideals or agree with our course of action. We believe strongly, however, that by fostering relationships with other agencies and participating in coordinated community responses, survivors benefit.

CARDV's approach to systems advocacy—organized advocacy to change policies—is to look for the points we can agree upon and build from there. We do not soften our mission to make it more acceptable. We view each interaction with our community partners as an opportunity to provide insight into the dynamics of sexual and domestic violence and the impact those dynamics may have on our mutual clients. We always, *always* stand with the survivor and support her in her choices.

Thirty-five years ago, when no one acknowledged the existence of sexual and domestic violence, the movement used blunt language and images to grab the public's attention and shock them into awareness. Domestic violence was

referred to as "battering" or "wife beating." The broad continuum of sexual assault was categorized under the head-
ing of "rape." As community awareness increased, so our
language evolved: "domestic violence" or "intimate partner violence" replaced "battering," and "sexual assault" is
more commonly used now. The posters that once depicted
bruised and defeated women have given way to the more
hopeful images of strong and powerful women.

Advocacy for survivors has shifted over the years as
well. In the earliest days, CARDV was almost entirely run
by volunteers possessing varying degrees of skill, with just
one or two paid staff for support. Survivors were encouraged to advocate for one another. As funding increased,
grantors expected more of agencies; and as the movement's
knowledge base grew, our own expectations of our service
delivery magnified. It would be very difficult for a volunteer coming in once or twice a week to keep up with all the
information that advocates are required to stay current with
now. Not that direct service volunteers don't continue to
contribute greatly to CARDV's work—supported by staff,
volunteers provide legal advocacy, answer our crisis and
support line, transport survivors to appointments, offer
respite childcare, and work in the shelters with residents.

Our work has always been from our hearts. That is
CARDV's professionalism.

~

It would be a lie to say that something hasn't been lost from
those long-ago chaotic days when CARDV was so new.
Perhaps because the work itself was still in its infancy and
not yet clearly defined, and there were so many of us who

were barely out of our own violent situations, the edges between the survivors and ourselves got blurred somehow. We were them.

Survivors meeting at our office or coming into shelter found themselves in the midst of a cluttered jumble of donated furniture, desks and file cabinets. Collages and glittered affirmations created by former residents competed for wall space with newspaper clippings, meeting announcements, posters, and rule reminders. There was a sense that many people had passed through these rooms before and many would follow. And that each one would leave something of herself behind for the next.

Today, the Advocacy Center, clean and beautiful and new, and the organized, well-maintained shelters impart a feeling of great respect for survivors and a sense of competence and order. It's doubtful, though, that a survivor believes she will be leaving anything of herself behind for the next person.

Instead, when a survivor leaves CARDV now, she goes with an understanding of the causes and dynamics of sexual and domestic violence and a comprehensive safety plan. She's plugged into the agencies that can assist her in her goals. She's aware of the other resources available to her in Linn and Benton counties, and that should this area prove to be unsafe for her, CARDV has the means to help her relocate. She knows that CARDV has a thorough knowledge of the system and can be counted on to advocate for her in the future. She's gained greater confidence in herself and her own capabilities.

Advocates today are wholly grounded in an understanding of CARDV's role in working with survivors. And their assuredness and competency imparts a sense of security to survivors as they go about the hard business of constructing a new life for themselves and their children.

The gains for survivors, and advocates as well, far outweigh any nostalgia for the old days.

∼

It is not possible to speak of CARDV and our work without acknowledging feminism. Feminism *is* our work and our work *is* feminism. Expanding opportunities for women — not telling them what to do or making choices for them — is feminism's bottom line.

And it is the heart of survivor-centered advocacy.

We listen carefully to understand the survivor's needs so we can offer support, and most importantly, safety plan with her. We make no judgments or assumptions about her circumstances and trust that she knows her situation best. We meet her where she is — intellectually, emotionally, at a safe physical location, and, if necessary, through an interpreter. We offer her information, resources, validation, encouragement, shelter, a 911 phone, a bus ticket out of town, groceries, diapers, whatever it is she needs in the moment. We support her decisions.

CARDV was founded in feminism and continues to operate as a feminist organization because women do not yet have the same economic, political and social rights and protections that men enjoy. Domestic violence, sexual assault, stalking, sex trafficking, and sexual harassment are still being used to maintain power and control over women.

There will come a day when domestic and sexual violence, in all its forms, is considered so abhorrent that perpetrators are unable to justify their actions and the public and legal system can no longer look the other way. It is towards that glorious day that CARDV continues to advocate for survivors through programs and services, fundraising and public awareness events, community education, the legal and justice system, and legislative changes.

Our name—the Center Against Rape and Domestic Violence—remains a political statement.

There are times in life when a person
has to rush off in pursuit of hopefulness.
Jean Giono

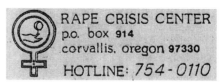

RAPE CRISIS CENTER
p.o. box 914
corvallis, oregon 97330
HOTLINE: 754-0110

LINN-BENTON ASSOCIATION
FOR THE PREVENTION OF
DOMESTIC VIOLENCE
850 S.W. 35th Street, Corvallis, Oregon 97330 — 758-0219

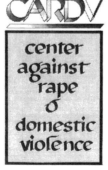

CARDV
center
against
rape
&
domestic
violence

Corvallis Gazette-Times

Spectrum

Rape hotline starts tonight

A telephone hotline for women who need emergency rape counseling or counseling for a past rape experience will become operational tonight at 7.

The telephone number is 754-0110. The telephone line will be open from 7 p.m. Fridays to 7 a.m. Sundays. Corvallis Women Against Rape, which is staffing the line, plans to keep it open more hours as soon as more counselors can be trained later this month or in February.

Mary Betts Sinclair, Corvallis Women Against Rape publicity chairman, says the organization has been planning for the hotline about one year but didn't have funding until now. It received $400 from a Portland women's organization and raised another $200 at garage sales.

Sinclair says the line is open to any woman who wants to call in about a rape or related problem. She says they expect more calls from women with past experiences to discuss than emergency calls. In the case of a rape that has just occurred, she says hotline counselors will take the woman to the hospital for a check-up if she wants to go, and will assist her in reporting the rape to the police, in bringing charges, and in other areas.

Last year six rapes were reported to the Corvallis Police Department, four of which were cleared by arrests. None were reported to the Benton County Sheriff's Office. However, Diana Armetis (formerly Terdin), rape counselor at Sunflower House, says she was counseling three or four women a month and had one or two new rape reports a month from Linn and Benton county women.

Corvallis Gazette-Times, Friday, January 14, 1977.

CWAR's hotline opened Friday evening, January 14, 1977. Operated entirely by volunteers, by 1980 the hotline was available 24-7.

Volunteer Opportunity

The Domestic Violence victim Advocate Program is seeking interested people to work with domestic violence victims and their children. Volunteer advocates give information, alternatives and support to victims of intra-family violence.

Advocate Training Includes:

* Information on Social Services and resources in Linn and Benton counties,
* An overview of the problem of domestic violence,
* Development of listening skills,
* Role Playing and Guest speakers,

We Invite Your Participation

For More Information Contact by Jan. 19th,

Debra Ross
Human Resource Center
850 SW 35th St,
Corvallis, Ore, 758-0219

Sponsored by the Linn Benton assoc. for the prevention of Domestic violence's Benton County Volunteer Services,

The Linn-Benton Association for the Prevention of Domestic Violence advertised for volunteers with hand-drawn flyers posted around town.

Rape-violence foes near purchase of 'safe house'

By Barbara Curtin
Of The Gazette-Times

Benton County women who are beaten by their spouses are one step closer to having a "safe house" in which to hide.

The Center Against Rape and Domestic Violence this week completed arrangements to buy a Corvallis house, using money loaned by the city. After necessary renovations are completed, the house should open in January, said Debra Ross, co-director of the center.

Once the shelter home is in operation, the group will be much more effective in helping victims of domestic violence, Ross said.

"We see women who have left home in the middle of the night, often with their children and only the clothing on their backs," she said. "They may need clothing, transportation and financial assistance. Typically, they have a lot of intense feelings and experiences that they need to sort out in a 'safe place.'"

The address of the house is not being disclosed, so that angry husbands or partners cannot follow the women who seek shelter there.

Until now, domestic violence victims have been placed temporarily with private families that volunteer to shelter them for a few days. However, there has been a serious need for a place where women can stay for longer periods, while they get their lives in order, Ross said.

The group purchased the house with a $150,000 loan from the city. The money came from the U.S. Housing and Urban Development's community development block grant program. The federal agency awards cities grants for projects that benefit low- and moderate-income people.

The center will have to repay the money if it ever sells the building or if the building ceases to be used as a "safe house."

"We hope to continue using the building indefinitely," Ross said.

Center representatives spent nine months looking for a suitable building.

"It's in fairly good shape," Ross said. "It has five bedrooms and it's light and airy. It's in a nice place for a shelter."

The group will have a contractor to do the renovations necessary to bring the building up to fire code standards. The city will loan up to $15,000 more, also from federal funds, to complete the remodeling, according to Ken Black, Corvallis community development coordinator.

The Rape Crisis Center and the Linn-Benton Association for Prevention of Domestic Violence have backed the shelter house project for several years. The two groups merged in July to form the Center Against Rape and Domestic Violence.

Working from an office at 219 S.W. Madison Ave., the group provides 24-hour crisis service to victims of rape and domestic violence in Linn and Benton counties. Their hotline number is 754-0110.

The group already has about 40 volunteers who have been trained to help women in crisis situations. They recently hired a child services coordinator to work with the children who are expected to come to the shelter home.

The center now needs donations of furniture and household items for the shelter home.

"We need furniture, appliances, clothing, linens, everything that you would need to furnish a large family home," Ross said. "We're trying to keep costs down as much as possible."

Those who have donations can call the center's business number, 758-0619.

Corvallis Gazette-Times, 1981.

Notes from June 1981 meeting. Our name, "Center Against Rape and Domestic Violence," was chosen because it was bold, direct, and a political statement.

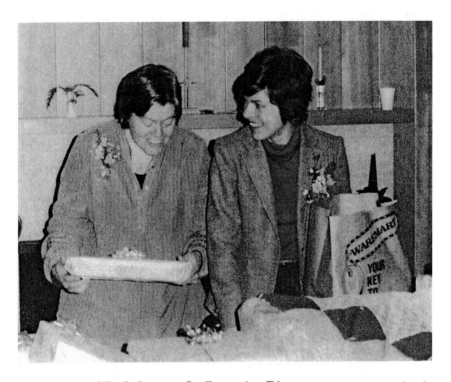

Deb Ross and Barb Sussex, Co-Executive Directors, open presents at the shower for CARDV's first shelter. January 10, 1982 at St. Mary's in Corvallis.

Living room in CARDV's first shelter, 1986.

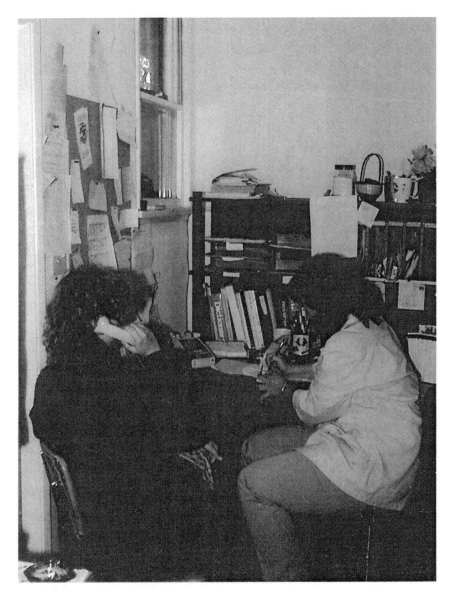

Advocate answers crisis line in staff area at CARDV's first shelter, 1986.

The Blake House in 1996. The Blake House, CARDV's first shelter, now serves as administrative offices.

Executive Director GayLynn Pack (on right) at the dedication of the
Pack House in 1997.

Christine Rhea, staff member, and Juanita Rodriguez, CARDV
board, at the Benton County Fair, 1995.

Hand drawn and colored posters advertised the Spaghetti Dinner in the 1980s.

Live music at the 2008 Spaghetti Dinner.

Staff members Mary Zelinka, Cybil Stockman, Wanda Terrell, and board member Jim Luebke serve up spaghetti at the 2005 Spaghetti Dinner.

CARDV's corn on the cob booth at the Fall Festival 1998.

Board member Carol Jauquet roasting corn on the cob at the Fall Festival 1998.

Clothesline Project exhibit at International Women's Day celebration
in Portland, 1994.

Winner of CARDV's first Poster Contest—Eric Gordon, Corvallis High School, 2006.

Plain Talk presentation at elementary school in 2005. CARDV incorporated Plain Talk into CARDV's Community Education Program in 2002.

Board Chair Barbara Balz at the 2005 Mother's Day Run/Walk for Safe Families.

Jim Luebke, board member and Albany Police Department officer, keeps traffic moving at the 2008 Mother's Day Run/Walk for Safe Families.

Stacy Mellem (wearing hat), volunteer race organizer, and her team at the 2008 Mother's Day Run/Walk for Safe Families. From left: Alannah Cooper, Katie Cooper, Katy Kuhert, Tonya Wells.

Crystal Kelley, CARDV's Events Director, and Oregon State University's Benny Beaver at the 2011 Mother's Day Run/Walk for Safe Families.

Lucy Daumen Casal, Volunteeer Coordinator, sets up for the Safe Families Breakfast, 2013.

Attorney General Hardy Myers presents Letetia Wilson, Crisis Response Advocate, with the 2007 Advocacy Award.

Cybil Stockman, Case Manager, is awarded the PASSION Award at the Oregon Coalition Against Domestic and Sexual Violence Conference, July 2009.

Nancy O'Mara, Executive Director, Debbie Bird McCubbin, Board Chair, and John Marchel, Board Treasurer, accept award for Nonprofit of the Year at the 2008 Celebrate Corvallis.

Nancy O'Mara, Executive Director 2001–10. (Photo courtesy of
Corvallis Gazette-Times.)

"Everyone Deserves to be Safe," 2014 Strawberry Festival in Lebanon. First place Non-profit Division and winner of the Grand Parade Sweepstakes.

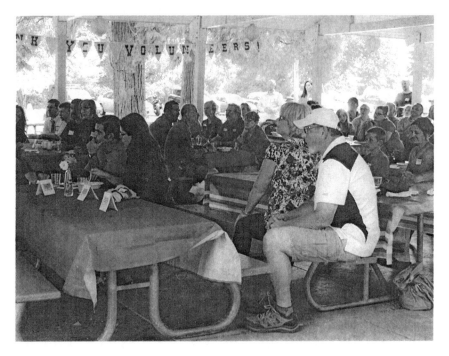

Volunteer Appreciation Picnic, August 2015.

Executive Director Letetia Wilson presents Board Treasurer
John Marchel with the Mary Zelinka Advocate for Social
Justice Award at the Annual Board Meeting, November
2015. The award was established in 2006 and is given
annually to a community member who has gone above
and beyond in their field to serve survivors.

Doug Marteeny, Linn County District Attorney, speaks in front of CARDV's 1 in 4 display at the Candlelight Vigil in Albany honoring those impacted by domestic violence on October 29, 2015. (Photo by Emagine Marketing & Photography.)

Candlelight Vigil in Albany, October 29, 2015.
(Photo by Emagine Marketing & Photography.)

Center Against Rape and Domestic Violence Advocacy Center at
Alexander Court, 2012.
(Photo by Mike Dean, photographer,
Bergsund-DeLaney Architecture)

Appendices

Power and Control Wheel

PHYSICAL **VIOLENCE** **SEXUAL**

USING COERCION AND THREATS
Making and/or carrying out threats to do something to hurt her • threatening to leave her, to commit suicide, to report her to welfare • making her drop charges • making her do illegal things.

USING INTIMIDATION
Making her afraid by using looks, actions, gestures • smashing things • destroying her property • abusing pets • displaying weapons.

USING ECONOMIC ABUSE
Preventing her from getting or keeping a job • making her ask for money • giving her an allowance • taking her money • not letting her know about or have access to family income.

USING EMOTIONAL ABUSE
Putting her down • making her feel bad about herself • calling her names • making her think she's crazy • playing mind games • humiliating her • making her feel guilty.

POWER AND CONTROL

USING MALE PRIVILEGE
Treating her like a servant • making all the big decisions • acting like the "master of the castle" • being the one to define men's and women's roles

USING ISOLATION
Controlling what she does, who she sees and talks to, what she reads, where she goes • limiting her outside involvement • using jealousy to justify actions.

USING CHILDREN
Making her feel guilty about the children • using the children to relay messages • using visitation to harass her • threatening to take the children away.

MINIMIZING, DENYING AND BLAMING
Making light of the abuse and not taking her concerns about it seriously • saying the abuse didn't happen • shifting responsibility for abusive behavior • saying she caused it.

PHYSICAL **VIOLENCE** **SEXUAL**

DOMESTIC ABUSE INTERVENTION PROJECT
202 East Superior Street
Duluth, Minnesota 55802
218-722-2781
www.duluth-model.org

Wheel of Equality

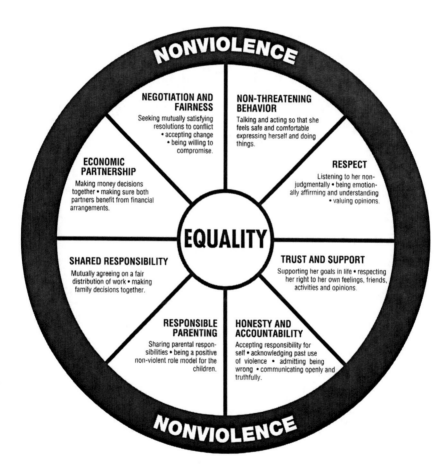

NONVIOLENCE

NEGOTIATION AND FAIRNESS
Seeking mutually satisfying resolutions to conflict • accepting change • being willing to compromise.

NON-THREATENING BEHAVIOR
Talking and acting so that she feels safe and comfortable expressing herself and doing things.

ECONOMIC PARTNERSHIP
Making money decisions together • making sure both partners benefit from financial arrangements.

RESPECT
Listening to her non-judgmentally • being emotionally affirming and understanding • valuing opinions.

EQUALITY

SHARED RESPONSIBILITY
Mutually agreeing on a fair distribution of work • making family decisions together.

TRUST AND SUPPORT
Supporting her goals in life • respecting her right to her own feelings, friends, activities and opinions.

RESPONSIBLE PARENTING
Sharing parental responsibilities • being a positive non-violent role model for the children.

HONESTY AND ACCOUNTABILITY
Accepting responsibility for self • acknowledging past use of violence • admitting being wrong • communicating openly and truthfully.

NONVIOLENCE

DOMESTIC ABUSE INTERVENTION PROJECT
202 East Superior Street
Duluth, Minnesota 55802
218-722-2781
www.duluth-model.org

The Center Against Rape and Domestic Violence

Mission Statement and Principles of Unity

MISSION STATEMENT

The mission of the Center Against Rape and Domestic Violence is two-fold:

To provide services and support to those affected by sexual and domestic violence, and

To provide education and leadership within the community to change the societal conditions that cultivate these forms of violence.

Principles of Unity

Victimization of Women

We believe that violence against women is endemic to our society. By "violence against women" we refer to both specific and general abuse of women and children. In addition to murder, rape, battering, sexual harassment, pornography and other forms of physical violence, it also includes attitudes and values that create and reproduce violence.

Freedom from Violation

We believe that all women, children and families have the right to live a life free of violence or the threat of violence. They have the right to freedom from violations of their personal autonomy and physical integrity on the street, in the home and at the workplace. To insure this, women should not have to restrict their freedom of movement, their bodies or their activities in order to be safe.

Self-Determination

We believe that all women have the right to make their own decisions regarding sexual and reproductive matters, lifestyles, finances, education and employment. We support women in this journey by providing a broad range of services to assist them in reaching their full potential.

Leadership in Education and Change

We believe that the root causes of violence against women stem from a belief in the supremacy of one sex over the other and are legitimated and reproduced by a complex series of institutional and social arrangements that define and treat women as subordinate. CARDV actively works to provide leadership and education in order to bring about the changes necessary in society to reduce this violence.

Religious Freedom

Religious beliefs and practices are a matter of personal conscience and individual choice, and a member shall neither promote nor discourage a particular religious belief in the course of her/his work.

Unity of Community

We believe classism, racism, ableism, heterosexism, ageism and other forms of elitism are systems and attitudes separating people from one another and interfere with the full use of our collective power base. CARDV does not condone these systems or attitudes either in our policies or in our individual practices. Our membership is open to individuals of all backgrounds. We further recognize that survivors of violence represent an essential constituency in our movement. We strongly encourage full participation by survivors, particularly by those women CARDV has sheltered.

Adopted December 3, 2001 by the Membership at CARDV's 2001 Annual Meeting.

Executive Directors

Linn-Benton Association for
the Prevention of Domestic Violence
Deb Ross: January 1980–July 1981

Rape Crisis Center
Barb Sussex: 1979–July 1981

CARDV
Deb Ross and Barb Sussex, co-directors: 1981–late fall 1983
Martha Clemons: January 1984–May 1984
Sara Deyo: May 1984–April 1987
Sarah Jordan: April 1987–March 1989
Sue Parrott: May 1989–August 1991
Barbara Jennings: August 1991–July 1992
GayLynn Pack: August 1992–April 3, 1998
Kit Miller (interim): May 1998–August 1998
Marvina Lepianka (interim): August 1998–February 1999
Tina Alexanderson: March 1999–May 2001
Ilene McClelland and Mary Zelinka (co-interims):
    May 2001–November 2001
Nancy O'Mara: November 2001–June 2010
Ann Kohler (interim): June 2010–October 2010

Toni Ryan: October 2010–March 2013

Letetia Wilson (interim): March 2013–September 2013

Letetia Wilson: September 2013–

Awards and Honors

CARDV

1989: Beyond War Foundation acknowledged CARDV for "demonstrating a model of commitment to solving crucial issues of our time, thereby helping to build our common future."

1991: Volunteer Action Committee of Benton County recognized CARDV for "outstanding service to the citizens of Benton County."

1997: Excellence in Community Services—awarded by the Oregon Housing and Community Services Department. Award is presented to "organizations that have made significant contributions in providing community services for lower income Oregonians." Nominated by the Governing Board of Community Services Consortium.

2008: Named Nonprofit of the Year at Celebrate Corvallis—the first time the Corvallis-Benton Chamber Coalition presented an award for Community Organization or Nonprofit of the Year.

2013: Recognized by The City of Corvallis Martin Luther King, Jr. Commission for providing "selfless service to the community in the spirit of the work of Dr. King."

2013: Volunteer Service Award, Partnership of the Year, from Boys and Girls Club of Corvallis. "In recognition and appreciation of your continued commitment to providing excellent volunteers in support of our local youth."

CARDV Staff, Board Members, Volunteers

Oregon Department of Justice, Crime Victims Assistance Unit—awarded by Attorney General Hardy Myers "In recognition of her valuable contribution to the field of victims' services and ongoing demonstration of the value of victims' rights."
   2007: Letetia Wilson

Oregon Coalition Against Domestic and Sexual Violence PASSION Awards
   "Recognizing outstanding advocates who exemplify the following qualities in support of their program's goals: Perseverance, Advocacy, Sensitivity, Strength, Integrity, Optimism, Nurturance."
   2004: Rachel VanDerlip, Case Manager
   2006: Letetia Wilson and Jenny Woodson,
   Crisis Response Advocates
   2009: Cybil Stockman, Case Manager

People Who Make a Difference: *Corvallis Gazette-Times* and *Albany Democrat-Herald*
>   2005: Nancy O'Mara, Executive Director
>   2013: Letetia Wilson, Executive Director

Women of Achievement: Oregon State University Women's Center
>   "Recognizing women for their commitment to equality and dedication to furthering the status of women in Oregon; and for work that has a wide impact and has potential for creating real change."
>   1992: Ataa A. Akyeampong,
>   CARDV Board of Directors
>   1994: Prudence Miles, former CARDV Staff
>   1997: GayLynn Pack, Executive Director CARDV
>   1999: Karyle Butcher, former CARDV
>   Board of Directors
>   1999: Mina McDaniel, CARDV Board of Directors
>   2000: Susan Shaw, CARDV Board of Directors
>   2003: Linda Klinge, former CARDV
>   Board of Directors
>   2004: Mary Zelinka, CARDV Staff
>   2004: Anisa Zvonkovic, former CARDV
>   Board of Directors
>   2005: Nancy O'Mara, Executive Director CARDV
>   2008: Debbie Bird McCubbin, CARDV
>   Board of Directors
>   2009: Jenny Woodson, CARDV Staff
>   2010: Lorena Reynolds, CARDV Board of Directors

CARDV Board of Directors

Pamela Miller
Pamela Neely
Shannon O'Boyle
Stan Robson
Charlotte Sinclair
Dr. Eldon Younger

Corvallis Women Against Rape (CWAR)

No official board minutes found. Signatures on various official documents:

Rev. John Hall
Diane Kahl
Laurie Hanson Murphy
Marlyss Schwengels Handy

Rape Crisis Center

No official board minutes found. Signatures on various official documents:

Maria Collins
Rev. John Hall
Marlyss Schwengels Handy
Laurie Hanson Murphy
Kristy Pope
Stan Robson

Center Against Rape and Domestic Violence

Following served on CARDV board during the fiscal years noted:

Melanie Adams: 2004–2005, 2005–2006, 2006–2007

Brie Akins: 2012–2013, 2013–2014, 2014–2015

Ataa Akyeampong: 1991–1992, 1992–1993

Anita Allen: 1986–1987, 1987–1988, 1988–1989

Mercedes Altizer: 1989–1990, 1990–1991

Cally Anderson: 1987–1988

Judith Armatta: 1981–1982, 1982–1983

Jaylene Badr: 1994–1995, 1995–1996

Walter Balk: 1994–1995, 1995–1996

Barbara Balz: 1998–1999, 1999–2000, 2000–2001, 2001–2002, 2002–2003, 2003–2004, 2004–2005, 2005–2006, 2006–2007

Gaylyn Bellegante: 1998–1999

Mary Bentley: 2006–2007, 2007–2008, 2008–2009, 2009–2010, 2010–2011, 2011–2012, 2012–2013, 2013–2014, 2014–2015, 2015–2016

Pat Berman: 1982–1983, 1983–1984, 1984–1985

Debbie Bird McCubbin: 2004–2005, 2005–2006, 2006–2007, 2007–2008, 2008–2009, 2009–2010, 2010–2011

Faye Blake: 1982–1983, 1983–1984, 1984–1985

Molly Bloomfield: 1984–1985, 1985–1986, 1986–1987, 1987–1988

Steve Blum: 1988–1989, 1989–1990

Brian Brown: 1991–1992, 1992–1993, 1993–1994

Heather Burton: 2004–2005, 2005–2006, 2006–2007, 2007–2008

Karyle Butcher: 1984–1985, 1985–1986, 1986–1987, 1987–1988

Donna Champeau: 2009–2010, 2010–2011, 2011–2012, 2012–2013, 2013–2014

Sidney Chase: 2002–2003, 2003–2004, 2004–2005, 2005–2006

Shoshana Cohen: 1991–1992, 1992–1993

Juliane Conrad: 2002–2003, 2003–2004

Marian Cope: 1985–1986, 1986–1987

Deb Copeland: 1985–1986

Katie Corthel: 1985–1986

Ione Crandell: 1986–1987

Leslie Dana-Frigault: 1983–1984, 1984–1985

Nancy Davila-Williams: 1999–2000, 2000–2001

Dani Davis: 2015–2016

Dr. John Davis: 1981–1982, 1982–1983, 1983–1984, 1984–1985, 1985–1986

Julie Davis: 2008–2009, 2009–2010, 2010–2011

Rita Davis: 1991–1992, 1992–1993

Eda Davis-Butts: 2005–2006, 2006–2007, 2007–2008

Mary Anne Deagan: 2011–2012, 2012–2013

Joan Demarest: 2006–2007, 2007–2008, 2008–2009

Carla Denner: 1998–1999, 1999–2000, 2000–2001, 2001–2002, 2002–2003, 2003–2004

Cynthia Dettman: 1982–1983, 1983–1984

Carol Dion: 2002–2003, 2003–2004, 2005–2006, 2006–2007

Dael Dixon-Coffee: 1983–1984, 1984–1985, 1985–1986

Coralee Edwards: 1984–1985, 1985–1986

Joe Elwood: 2011–2012, 2012–2013, 2013–2014, 2014–2015, 2015–2016

Sue Erekson: 1981–1982, 1982–1983, 1983–1984, 1984–1985, 1985–1986

Ellen Ferregro: 1989–1990

Pam Folts: 1990–1991, 1991–1992

Laurie Frys: 1985–1986

Nikki Garrett-Black: 2005–2006

Sue Gifford: 1994–1995, 1995–1996

Cheryl Glenn: 1994–1995

Erlinda Gonzales-Berry: 2004–2005, 2005–2006

Gretchen Goode: 2013–2014, 2014–2015

Ellen Gradison: 1988–1989, 1989–1990, 1990–1991, 1991–1992

Kathleen Greaves: 1993–1994, 1994–1995

George Grosch: 2007–2008

Judy Hadley: 1982–1983, 1983–1984, 1984–1985

Lani Haire: 1986–1987

Nancy Hall: 1986–1987

Rita Hamann: 2010–2011, 2011–2012

Susan Hamill: 1986–1987, 1987–1988

Barb Hansen: 1992–1993, 1993–1994

Dan Hendrickson: 2008–2009, 2009–2010, 2010–2011, 2011–2012, 2012–2013, 2013–2014

Kay Ellen Hones: 1983–1984

Wayne Hyde: 1988–1989, 1989–1990, 1990–1991

Deborah Jacobs: 1983–1984, 1984–1985, 1985–1986, 1986–1987, 1987–1988

Carol A. Jauquet: 1995–1996, 1996–1997, 1997–1998, 1998–1999

Ron Johnston: 1987–1988, 1988–1989, 1989–1990

Kristen Jones: 2004–2005, 2005–2006, 2006–2007, 2007–2008, 2008–2009, 2009–2010, 2010–2011, 2011–2012

Sarah Jordan: 1984–1985

Barry Kerr: 2002–2003

Linda Klinge: 1991–1992, 1992–1993

Dottie Koehrsen: 1990–1991

Carol Koppenstein: 1998–1999, 1999–2000
Judith Kuipers: 1981–1982, 1982–1983
Marie Laper: 1998–1999, 1999–2000, 2000–2001
Susan Lax: 1992–1993, 1993–1994, 1994–1995
Cindy Lindner: 1987–1988, 1988–1989, 1989–1990
Susan Linson: 1981–1982
Scott Logan: 1996–1997, 1997–1998, 1998–1999, 1999–
    2000, 2000–2001, 2001–2002, 2002–2003, 2003–2004,
    2004–2005, 2005–2006
Jim Luebke: 2000–2001, 2001–2002, 2002–2003, 2003–
    2004, 2004–2005, 2005–2006, 2006 2007, 2007–2008,
    2008–2009, 2009–2010, 2010–2011, 2011–2012,
    2012–2013, 2013–2014, 2014–2015, 2015–2016
Gloria Lundin: 1985–1986
Cynthia MacKay: 1995–1996, 1996–1997, 1997–1998,
    1998–1999
Lupe Maginnis: 1988–1989, 1989–1990, 1990–1991
John Marchel: 2002–2003, 2003–2004, 2004–2005, 2005–
    2006, 2006–2007, 2007–2008, 2008–2009, 2009–2010,
    2010–2011, 2011–2012, 2012–2013, 2013–2014,
    2014–2015, 2015–2016
Nancy Marshall: 1991–1992, 1992–1993, 1993–1994,
    1994–1995
Art Martinak: 1982–1983, 1983–1984, 1984–1985,
    1985–1986, 1986–1987, 1987–1988
Arb Matyas: 1981–1982
Mina McDaniel: 1988–1989, 1989–1990, 1990–1991,
    1991–1992, 1992–1993, 1993–1994, 1994–1995, 1995–
    1996, 1996–1997, 1997–1998, 1998–1999, 1999–2000,
    2000–2001, 2001–2002, 2002–2003, 2003–2004
Kara McDonald: 2014–2015, 2015–2016

Mealoha McFadden: 2005–2006, 2006–2007, 2014–2015, 2015–2016

Barb McGuire: 1981–1982, 1982–1983

Kati McLellan: 1989–1990, 1990–1991

Donna Meyer: 1981–1982

Kit Miller: 1996–1997, 1997–1998

Maggi Milton: 1991–1992, 1992–1993

Sherry Moore: 1986–1987

Tarek Murtada: 1996–1997, 1997–1998

Dianne Myers: 1986–1987

Aisha Nasser: 2012–2013, 2013–2014, 2014–2015, 2015–2016

Karuna Neustadt: 1986–1987, 1987–1988, 1988–1989, 1989–1990, 1990–1991

Jennifer Nitson: 2008–2009, 2009–2010, 2010–2011, 2011–2012, 2012–2013, 2013–2014, 2014–2015

Cynthia Noble: 2013–2014, 2014–2015, 2015–2016

Phyllis Nofziger: 1987–1988

Steve Oldenstadt: 1991–1992

Nana Osei-Kofi: 2014–2015, 2015–2016

Lori Palmquist: 1991–1992, 1992–1993, 1993–1994, 1994–1995

Mary Parker: 2003–2004, 2004–2005, 2005–2006, 2006–2007

Gina Pastega: 2007–2008, 2008–2009, 2009–2010

Ellen Perreard: 1990–1991

Kathleen Petrucela: 2009–2010, 2010–2011, 2011–2012, 2012–2013, 2013–2014, 2014–2015, 2015–2016

Keri Phipps: 1983–1984, 1984–1985

Grace Pittman: 1989–1990, 1991–1992, 1992–1993, 1993–1994, 1994–1995, 1995–1996, 1996–1997, 1997–1998, 1998–1999, 1999–2000, 2000–2001, 2001–2002

Nancy Powell: 1986–1987, 1994–1995, 1995–1996

Theresa Reinhardt: 1988–1989, 1989–1990

Lorena Reynolds: 1999–2000, 2000–2001, 2001–2002, 2002–2003, 2003–2004, 2004–2005, 2005–2006, 2007–2008, 2008–2009, 2009–2010, 2010–2011, 2011–2012, 2012–2013, 2013–2014, 2014–2015

Tammy Rider: 1982–1983, 1983–1984

Beth Rietveld: 2006–2007, 2007–2008, 2008–2009, 2009–2010, 2010–2011, 2011–2012

Wendy P. Rielly Thorson: 1996–1997, 1997–1998, 1998–1999, 1999–2000

Marian Roberts: 1987–1988, 1988–1989, 1989–1990, 1990–1991, 1992–1993, 1993–1994, 1994–1995

Lynne Robertson: 2003–2004

Stan Robson: 1981–1982, 1982–1983, 1983–1984, 1984–1985, 1985–1986, 1986–1987, 1987–1988, 1988–1989, 1989–1990, 1990–1991

Juanita Rodriguez: 1992–1993, 1993–1994, 1994–1995, 1995–1996, 1996–1997, 1997–1998, 1998–1999

Friah Rogers: 2006–2007, 2007–2008

Kristen Sager-Kottre: 2010–2011, 2011–2012

Jeannie Salyer: 1994–1995

Patti Sasseen: 1986–1987

Joe Scott: 2015–2016

Mary Alice Seville: 2007–2008, 2008–2009, 2009–2010, 2010–2011, 2011–2012, 2012–2013

Susan Shaw: 1999–2000, 2000–2001, 2001–2002, 2002–2003, 2003–2004, 2004–2005, 2005–2006, 2006–2007, 2007–2008, 2008–2009

Ray Shimabuku: 2000–2001, 2001–2002, 2002–2003, 2003–2004, 2004–2005

Mehra Shirazi: 2008–2009, 2009–2010, 2010–2011,
    2011–2012, 2012–2013, 2013–2014, 2014–2015
Jeannie Shyam: 1984–1985, 1985–1986
Charlotte Sinclair: 1981–1982, 1982–1983, 1983–1984,
    1984–1985
Jane Snyder: 2000–2001, 2001–2002, 2003–2004,
    2004–2005, 2005–2006
Mary Spide: 1981–1982
Cynthia Solie: 1989–1990, 1990–1991, 1991–1992, 1992–
    1993, 1993–1994, 1994–1995, 1995–1996, 1996–1997,
    1997–1998, 1998–1999, 1999–2000
Angie Stambuck-Simon: 2006–2007, 2007–2008
Shelley Stark: 1999–2000, 2000–2001
Faye Stetz-Waters: 2015–2016
Kathy Summerlin: 1981–1982
Kate Sundstrom: 2012–2013, 2013–2014, 2014–2015
Kamran Tahmaseb: 1991–1992, 1992–1993, 1993–1994
Diane Thies: 1982–1983
Toni Thomas Carroll: 2015–2016
Clair Thompson: 2010–2011, 2011–2012, 2012–2013,
    2013–2014
Andrea Thornberry: 2013–2014, 2014–2015, 2015–2016
David Visiko: 2000–2001, 2001–2002, 2002–2003
Ellen Volmert: 1996–1997, 1997–1998, 1998–1999,
    1999–2000, 2000–2001
Susan Wagner: 1981–1982
Lindy Walsh: 1981–1982, 1982–1983
Jessica White: 2002–2003, 2003–2004
Dessie Williams: 1999–2000, 2000–2001, 2001–2002
Jule Wind: 1986–1987, 1987–1988

Lori Wolcott: 1998–1999, 1999–2000, 2000–2001,
    2001–2002, 2002–2003
Barb Wood: 1991–1992, 1992–1993
Mary Zelinka: 1982–1983, 1983–1984
Cecilia Zoeller: 1996–1997, 1997–1998, 1998–1999,
    1999–2000
Karen Zorn: 1985–1986, 1986–1987, 1987–1988
Anisa Zvonkovic: 1990–1991, 1991–1992, 1992–1993,
    1993–1994, 1994–1995, 1995–1996, 1996–1997

Acknowledgments

One of the things I like best about working at CARDV is having the opportunity to meet and work with so many extraordinary people. Survivors (especially the survivors), co-workers, volunteers, board members, donors, community partners, funders—all have in some way impacted my worldview, and, I believe, made me a better person. Thank you.

Thank you to everyone who enthusiastically contributed to this project through spirited discussions, reminiscing, and answering my endless questions.

Specifically I wish to thank:

Interviewees: Judith Armatta, Bonnie Braeutigam, Karyle Butcher, Jim Luebke, Donna Meyer, Mary Rebar, Deb Ross, Marcia Shaw, Til Tillitson, Alice Vachss, and Letetia Wilson

First readers: Lynn Bain, Bonnie Braeutigam, Lucy Daumen Casal, Cybil Stockman, Alice Vachss, and Julie Weitzel.

Sybil Hebb, Director of Legislative Advocacy at the Oregon Law Center for her assistance with the Legislation portion of Part Two: Operations.

Cybil Stockman, for giving me the perfect title for this book.

Jennifer Nitson, for copy editing.

Meadowlark Publishing Services, for turning my manuscript into a real book.

To Judith Armatta and the memory of Barb Sussex: my profound gratitude for introducing me to what became my life's work. Your unwavering trust helped convince me that I was more than what had been done to me.

Center Against Rape and Domestic Violence: A Local History of a National Movement was researched and written entirely on my personal time and was published thanks to generous donations from: Donna Dimski Gilg, Sheila Duranso, Germaine Hammon, Meadowlark Publishing Services, Marsha Swanson, Wanda Terrell, and Cindy Towne.

One hundred percent of the proceeds from the sale of this book will benefit survivors of sexual and domestic violence.

Resources

The bulk of *Center Against Rape and Domestic Violence: A Local History of a National Movement's* background came from training materials, fact sheets, newsletters, grant proposals, and board of directors meeting minutes from Corvallis Women Against Rape, the Rape Crisis Center, Linn Benton Association for the Prevention of Domestic Violence, and the Center Against Rape and Domestic Violence. Additional resources were newspaper articles from the *Corvallis Gazette-Times, Albany Democrat-Herald, Lebanon Express,* OSU *Daily Barometer,* and the LBCC *Commuter.* These source materials spanned the years from 1976 to the time of publication.

I drew heavily on my own memories and those of the individuals I interviewed. Any errors or misinterpretations are entirely my own.

Interviewees:

Judith Armatta—CARDV co-founder and CARDV Board
of Directors, 1981–1983.

Bonnie Braeutigam—Domestic Violence/Sexual Assault
Fund Coordinator, Oregon Department of Human
Services, 1985–2009.

Karyle Butcher—CARDV Board of Directors, 1984–1988.

Jim Luebke—Linn-Benton Association for the Prevention
of Domestic Violence volunteer, 1979.

Donna Meyer—Linn-Benton Association for the
Prevention of Domestic Violence Board of Directors,
and CARDV Board of Directors, 1981–1982.

Mary Rebar—CARDV staff, 1989–1991.

Deb Ross—Director of Linn-Benton Association for the
Prevention of Domestic Violence and CARDV Co-
Director with Barb Sussex, 1981–1982.

Marcia Shaw—Safe House Host for Linn-Benton
Association for the Prevention of Domestic Violence,
1979–1981.

Til Tillitson—CARDV staff, 1981–1983.

Alice Vachss—Chief of the Special Victims Bureau of the
Queens (NYC) District Attorney's Office, 1982–1991,
Author of *Sex Crimes*.

Letetia Wilson—CARDV Executive Director.

The following resources also helped inform *The Center Against Rape and Domestic Violence: A Local History of a National Movement.*

ARTICLES:

Aronson, Amy, "Outrageous Acts and Bad, Bad Girls." *Ms. Magazine* July/August 1998.

Bellafante, Ginia, "Feminism: It's All About Me!" *Time Magazine* June 29, 1998.

Column "How We Got Here." *Ms. Magazine* May/June 1995.

Coucher, Mimi, "There was a Life Before Feminism, But it Wasn't Pretty." *Bust Magazine* Winter 2000.

Edgar, Joanne, "Bring Men into the Conversation." *Ms. Magazine* Summer 2002.

Faludi, Susan, "Looking Beyond the Slogans." *Newsweek Magazine* December 28, 1992.

Flood, Michael, "Claims about Husband Battering." Domestic Violence and Incest Resource Center (www.ncdsv.org) 1999.

Gates, David, "White Male Paranoia." *Newsweek Magazine* March 29, 1993.

Gibbs, Nancy, "The War Against Feminism." *Time Magazine* March 9, 1992.

Hauser, Susan G., "The Women's Movement in the '70s, Today: You've Come a Long Way, But." Workforce (www.workforce.com).

Isaacson, Walter, "Who Mattered and Why." *Time Magazine* December 31, 1999.

Jacklet, Ben, "The Secret Watchers." *Portland Tribune* September 12, 2002.

Lehrner, Amy, and Allen, Nicole E., "Still a Movement After All These Years?" *Violence Against Women.* Sage Publications 2009.

Laurel Paulson, "Women and Justice: The Vindication of Charity Lamb." *Oregon Encyclopedia, Oregon History and Culture* (www.oregonencyclopedia.org).

Panel discussion, "Let's Get Real About Feminism." *Ms. Magazine* September/October 1993.

Panel discussion, "Real Men Join the Movement." *Ms. Magazine* November/December 1997.

Pence, Ellen, "Advocacy on Behalf of Battered Women." *Violence Against Women* 2001. Sage Publications.

Pruett, Holly Jane, "A Feminist Family Album." *Ms. Magazine* March/April 1992.

Shulman, Alix Kates, "Feminism Then and Now." *The Sun Magazine* June 1998.

Steinem, Gloria, "Advice to Old Feminists." *Ms. Magazine* February/March 2000.

BOOKS:

Brownmiller, Susan, *Against Our Will: Men, Women and Rape.* Simon and Schuster 1975.

Brownmiller, Susan, *In Our Time: Memoir of a Revolution.* Random House 1999.

Faludi, Susan, *Backlash: The Undeclared War Against American Women.* Crown Publishers, Inc. 1991.

hooks, bell, *Feminism is for Everybody.* Pluto Press 2000.

Katz, Jackson, *The Macho Paradox — Why Some Men Hurt Women and How All Men Can Help.* Sourcebooks, Inc. 2006.

Kilbourne, Jean, *Can't Buy My Love.* Touchstone 1999.

Krakauer, Jon, *Missoula.* Doubleday 2015.

Martin, Del, *Battered Wives*. Glide 1976.

Sherr, Lynn, *Failure is Impossible*. Times Books 1996.

Vachss, Alice, *Sex Crimes*. Random House 1993.

PERIODICALS:

Ms. Magazine special issues:

    No More! Stopping Domestic Violence, September/
October 1994.

    25 Years, September/October 1997.

    Feminism: Celebrating the First Century, December/
January 1999/2000.

    The Best of 30 Years, Spring 2002.

    40th Anniversary Issue, Fall 2012.

NEWSLETTERS, FACT SHEETS, WEBINARS:

Braeutigam, Bonnie "MLT History" and "Brief Timeline of
Domestic and Sexual Assault Services and Funding in
Oregon."

Corvallis NOW Newsletter, October 1995.

Equity Allocation Study Developed for CPS Unit,
Children, Adults and Families—DHS and Crime
Victims Assistance Section of the Oregon
Department of Justice, June 2006.

Family Violence Prevention and Services Act Webinar,
October 9, 2014.

Mid-Valley Crisis Services Newsletter, Summer 1996.

Oregon Coalition Against Domestic and Sexual Violence various training materials and fact sheets, 1989–current.

Oregon SART Handbook, November 2002.

WEBSITES:

American Association of University Women—
www.aauw.org

American Civil Liberties Union—www.aclu.org

Bust Magazine—www.bust.com

Community Outreach, Inc.—www.communityout-reachinc.org

Crime Victims Services Division—www.doj.state.or.us

Duluth (Minnesota) Domestic Abuse Intervention Project—www.theduluthmodel.org

Indiana Coalition Against Domestic Violence—
www.icadvinc.org

Minnesota Center Against Violence and Abuse—
www.mincava.umn.edu

Ms. Magazine—www.msmagazine.com

National Coalition Against Domestic Violence—
www.ncadv.org

National Sexual Violence Resource Center—
www.nsvrc.org

Office for Victims of Crime—www.ovc.gov

Office on Violence Against Women—
www.justice.gov/ovw

Oregon Alliance to End Violence Against Women—
www.alliancetoendviolenceagainst women.org

Oregon Coalition Against Domestic and Sexual
    Violence—www.ocadsv.org
Oregon State University Women's Center—
    dce.oregonstate.edu/wc
Praxis International—www.praxisinternational.org
Washington Coalition Against Domestic Violence—
    www.wscadv.org
Washington Coalition of Sexual Assault Programs—
    www.wcsap.org

Mary Zelinka at CARDV's
twenty-fifth anniversary
celebration in 2006. At that
event CARDV established the
*Mary Zelinka Advocate for Social
Justice Award* to be given annually to a community member
who has gone above and
beyond in their field to
serve survivors.

About the Author

Mary Zelinka began advocacy work at the Rape Crisis Center in 1980, not long after leaving her violent husband in Colorado. She volunteered until 1984 when her employer transferred her to California. There she was active at the Sacramento Rape Crisis Center and served on the board of directors for Women Escaping a Violent Environment, Sacramento's domestic violence agency. In 1989 she returned to the Willamette Valley and CARDV's volunteer program. A year later she joined CARDV's staff as a part-time overnight advocate. In 1995, wanting to make advocacy work a larger part of her life, she left her full-time employer and transitioned into a daytime position at CARDV. Over the years she has served in a variety of different roles.

CPSIA information can be obtained at www.ICGtesting.com
Printed in the USA
LVOW10s0412180516

488730LV00007B/7/P

9 780997 540505